Contents Table

Welcome & What You'll Learn

Welcome, intrepid JavaScript explorer! If you're reading this, you likely have some experience with JavaScript, the versatile and sometimes perplexing language that powers the modern web. You might have dabbled in basic scripting, perhaps creating interactive elements or simple animations. But now, you're ready to venture beyond the basics, to dive deeper into the intricate mechanisms and sometimes quirky behaviors that make JavaScript both challenging and incredibly powerful.

Why This Book?

There are countless books and tutorials on JavaScript. So, why this one? Here's what sets "JavaScript: Beyond the Basics – Master the Quirks" apart:

- **Quirks Embraced:** Many resources shy away from JavaScript's peculiarities. This book dives right in, explaining the "why" behind the oddities and showing you how to harness them.
- **Depth and Practicality:** We won't just skim the surface. We'll explore concepts like scope, closures, prototypes, and the enigmatic `this` keyword in detail, with plenty of hands-on examples.
- **Building Your Own Tools:** You'll learn to leverage your newfound knowledge to build your own JavaScript frameworks and tools, giving you a deeper understanding of how the language works under the hood.
- **Modern and Future-Ready:** We'll cover essential modern JavaScript practices (ES6+) and peek into the future with upcoming features and trends.

Your Journey Ahead

This book is your roadmap to JavaScript mastery. Here's a glimpse of what you'll learn:

- **Section I: Foundations for the Journey:** We'll solidify your understanding of JavaScript's core building blocks: variables, data types, operators, expressions, and flow control.
- **Section II: Objects: The Heart of JavaScript:** We'll explore objects, prototypes, and inheritance, uncovering the mechanisms that make JavaScript's object model so flexible.
- **Section III: Deep Dive into Scope and Closures:** Prepare to conquer two of JavaScript's most important and often misunderstood concepts: scope and closures.
- **Section IV: Building Your Own JavaScript Tools:** Roll up your sleeves and put your knowledge to the test by creating a JavaScript framework from scratch.
- **Section V: Advanced JavaScript Techniques:** We'll delve into asynchronous JavaScript, functional programming techniques, and object-oriented programming in JavaScript.
- **Section VI: Putting it All Together:** We'll explore real-world use cases, debugging strategies, and the future of JavaScript.

Who Should Read This Book?

This book is perfect for you if:

- You have a basic understanding of JavaScript and want to level up.
- You're curious about the "why" behind JavaScript's unique behaviors.
- You want to build robust and efficient JavaScript applications.
- You're eager to learn how to create your own JavaScript libraries and frameworks.

Let's Get Started!

Are you ready to unlock the full potential of JavaScript? Turn the page, and let's embark on this exciting journey together!

Section I:
Foundations for the Journey

The Quirks of JavaScript: Why Understanding the "Weird Parts" is Key

Outline

- What Makes JavaScript Unique?
- Embracing the Quirks: Why They Matter
- Zero-Based Numbering and Automatic Semicolon Insertion
- Loose Typing and Type Coercion
- The Global Object and Hoisting
- Function Hoisting and Variable Hoisting
- The Infamous `this` Keyword
- The Prototype Chain and Prototypal Inheritance
- Chapter Summary

What Makes JavaScript Unique?

JavaScript's story began in 1995 as a simple scripting language designed to add interactivity to static web pages. Brendan Eich, working at Netscape, created it in just 10 days with the initial name "Mocha," later renamed "LiveScript," and finally, "JavaScript." This whirlwind development set the stage for JavaScript's rapid evolution.

Web Development Dominance

JavaScript's primary role has always been in web development. It's the language that brings web pages to life, enabling:

- **Dynamic Content:** Updating web page elements without full page reloads.
- **User Interaction:** Responding to clicks, hovers, and other user actions.
- **Animations and Visual Effects:** Creating engaging visual experiences.
- **Data Communication:** Sending and receiving data from web servers.

Beyond the Browser

While the web remains its core domain, JavaScript's versatility has allowed it to expand into other realms:

- **Server-Side Programming (Node.js):** Node.js brought JavaScript to the server, enabling the creation of scalable and efficient network applications.
- **Mobile Development (React Native):** React Native allows developers to build native mobile apps using JavaScript and React, a popular JavaScript library.
- **Desktop Applications (Electron):** Electron uses JavaScript, HTML, and CSS to build cross-platform desktop applications like Visual Studio Code and Slack.
- **Internet of Things (IoT):** JavaScript is increasingly used to program IoT devices due to its lightweight nature and event-driven model.

Key Distinguishing Features

Several key features make JavaScript stand out from other programming languages:

- **Dynamic Typing:** Variables in JavaScript can hold values of any data type, and their types can change at runtime. This flexibility allows for rapid development but requires careful attention to data validation.
- **Prototypal Inheritance:** JavaScript uses a unique inheritance model based on prototypes, which are objects that serve as blueprints for creating other objects. This model differs from the class-based inheritance found in languages like Java or C++.
- **First-Class Functions:** Functions in JavaScript are treated as first-class citizens, meaning they can be assigned to variables, passed as arguments to other functions, and returned from functions. This enables powerful functional programming patterns.
- **Event-Driven, Single-Threaded:** JavaScript's execution model is event-driven and single-threaded. This means it responds to events (like user clicks) and executes code in a single sequence, relying on asynchronous operations and callbacks to handle tasks that take time (like network requests).

In summary, JavaScript's rapid rise from a simple scripting language to a ubiquitous technology across web, mobile, desktop, and even IoT is a testament to its unique blend of features, flexibility, and the passionate community that continues to drive its evolution.

Embracing the Quirks: Why They Matter

JavaScript has earned a reputation for being "weird" or "quirky." For newcomers, encountering unexpected behaviors and results can be frustrating. Experienced developers from other languages might find JavaScript's syntax and paradigms unfamiliar. However, what may initially seem like quirks are, in fact, intentional design choices that empower JavaScript with its unique capabilities.

The Beauty of Flexibility

JavaScript's flexibility is a double-edged sword. It allows for quick and creative solutions, but it also means you need to be mindful of potential pitfalls. For example:

- **Loose Typing:** While dynamic typing enables rapid prototyping, it can lead to unexpected type conversions if you're not careful.
- **Automatic Semicolon Insertion:** This feature can sometimes mask errors, making debugging more challenging.
- **The `this` Keyword:** Its context-dependent nature can lead to unexpected behavior if you don't understand how it works.

Quirks as Opportunities

Rather than viewing these aspects as flaws, consider them opportunities for mastery. Understanding and embracing JavaScript's quirks will unlock a deeper level of proficiency.

- **Dynamic Typing:** Embrace the ability to write expressive code that adapts to different data types. Learn to use type checking tools to catch potential errors early.
- **Automatic Semicolon Insertion:** Adopt consistent coding practices and use linters to ensure your code is well-formatted and free of potential ASI-related issues.
- **The `this` Keyword:** Master the different binding mechanisms and use them to your advantage to write flexible and reusable code.

Writing Better Code

By delving into the "why" behind JavaScript's quirks, you'll gain the following benefits:

- **Fewer Bugs:** You'll be less likely to encounter unexpected behavior and spend less time debugging.
- **Cleaner Code:** You'll write code that's more predictable, maintainable, and easier for others to understand.
- **Greater Confidence:** You'll tackle complex JavaScript concepts with greater confidence and clarity.

A Journey of Understanding

This book is your guide to unraveling JavaScript's mysteries. By exploring each quirk in detail, you'll transform initial confusion into confident mastery. Remember, the "weird parts" are not roadblocks; they're stepping stones on your path to becoming a proficient JavaScript developer.

Zero-Based Numbering and Automatic Semicolon Insertion

Zero-based numbering and automatic semicolon insertion (ASI) are two fundamental aspects of JavaScript that can trip up newcomers. Understanding them is crucial to writing reliable code.

Zero-Based Numbering: The Foundation of Access

In JavaScript, arrays and strings are zero-indexed. This means the first element has an index of 0, the second element has an index of 1, and so on.

```
const numbers = [5, 12, 8, 130, 44];
console.log(numbers[0]); // Output: 5
console.log(numbers[4]); // Output: 44
```

Similarly, for strings:

```
const greeting = "Hello";
console.log(greeting[0]); // Output: H
console.log(greeting[4]); // Output: o
```

Zero-based numbering is the backbone of element access. It underpins iteration, slicing, and various string and array manipulations. Ignoring it leads to off-by-one errors.

Automatic Semicolon Insertion (ASI): A Double-Edged Sword

JavaScript has a feature called automatic semicolon insertion (ASI). It attempts to fix missing semicolons by adding them automatically. This can be convenient but also hazardous.

```
function sayHello() {
  return // ASI assumes a semicolon here
  "Hello!"
}
console.log(sayHello()); // Output: undefined
```

The intended behavior is lost because ASI inserted a semicolon after `return`. To fix this, always add semicolons explicitly:

```
function sayHello() {
  return "Hello!"; // Explicit semicolon
}
```

ASI Pitfalls: More Than Meets the Eye

ASI can cause other unexpected problems, especially with:

- **Return Statements:** Always place return values on the same line as `return`.
- **Immediately Invoked Function Expressions (IIFEs):** Wrap IIFEs in parentheses to avoid issues with preceding lines.
- **Multiple Statements on One Line:** Avoid this practice as ASI might not insert semicolons correctly.

Here's a subtle example:

```
const x = 1
[1, 2, 3].forEach(x => console.log(x)) // ASI can cause problems here
```

ASI might insert a semicolon after `x = 1`, leading to unexpected results. Adding semicolons explicitly or using separate lines prevents such issues.

Semicolons: Your Safety Net

While some developers advocate for omitting semicolons, adhering to a consistent semicolon style is a safer practice, especially in larger projects. It makes your code more predictable, easier to maintain, and less prone to ASI-related surprises.

Loose Typing and Type Coercion

One of JavaScript's defining characteristics is its loose typing system. Unlike languages like Java or C++, where you explicitly declare a variable's type, JavaScript variables can hold values of any data type. This flexibility is both a strength and a potential source of confusion.

Loose Typing: The Shape-Shifter

In JavaScript, you declare variables using `var`, `let`, or `const`. The same variable can hold different types of data throughout its lifetime:

```
let x = 5;      // x is a number
x = "Hello";    // x is now a string
x = true;       // x is now a boolean
```

This dynamism is convenient for rapid development, but it also requires vigilance.

Type Coercion: The Silent Transformer

JavaScript's loose typing goes hand in hand with type coercion. This is the automatic conversion of values from one data type to another when they're used in operations or comparisons. While sometimes helpful, type coercion can lead to unexpected results if you're not aware of it.

Examples of Type Coercion

1. Arithmetic Operations:

```
console.log("5" + 2);     // Output: "52" (string concatenation)
console.log("5" - 2);     // Output: 3 (string converted to number)
console.log("Hello" - 5); // Output: NaN (Not a Number)
```

2. Comparisons:

```
console.log(0 == false);    // Output: true (boolean coerced to number)
console.log(null == undefined); // Output: true (special case)
console.log("5" == 5);     // Output: true (number coerced to string)
```

```
console.log("5" === 5);    // Output: false (strict equality, no coercion)
```

Best Practices to Avoid Errors

To prevent unexpected outcomes due to type coercion, follow these best practices:

1. **Use Strict Equality (=== and !==):** These operators check both the value and the type, avoiding unwanted type conversions.
2. **Explicit Type Conversion:** When you need to convert types, use functions like `parseInt()`, `parseFloat()`, `Number()`, `String()`, or `Boolean()`.
3. **Understand Truthy and Falsy Values:** Be aware of which values are considered truthy (e.g., "Hello", 1, true) and which are falsy (e.g., "", 0, false, null, undefined) in JavaScript. This is especially important in conditional statements.
4. **Validate User Input:** When dealing with user input, always validate and sanitize the data to ensure you're working with the expected types.

By understanding loose typing and type coercion, you'll be better equipped to write predictable and reliable JavaScript code.

The Global Object and Hoisting

In JavaScript, the global object serves as the root of the scope chain and provides a container for globally accessible variables and functions. Understanding the global object and the concept of hoisting is crucial for writing well-structured and error-free code.

The Global Object: Your JavaScript Universe

In web browsers, the global object is the `window` object. It represents the browser window and provides access to various browser-related features like the DOM, timers, and events. In Node.js, the global object is named `global`.

Any variable or function declared in the global scope automatically becomes a property of the global object:

```
// In a browser environment
var myGlobalVar = 42;
function myGlobalFunction() {
  console.log("Hello from the global function!");
}

console.log(window.myGlobalVar);                    // Output: 42
window.myGlobalFunction();                           // Output: "Hello from the global
function!"
```

Hoisting: The JavaScript Time Machine

Hoisting is a JavaScript behavior where variable and function declarations are conceptually moved to the top of their scope before code execution. This means you can use a variable or function before its declaration in the code.

Function Hoisting: Functions First

Function declarations are fully hoisted, meaning you can call a function before it's declared in your code:

```
sayHello(); // Output: "Hello!"
```

```
function sayHello() {
  console.log("Hello!");
}
```

Variable Hoisting: Declarations Only

Variable declarations using `var` are also hoisted, but only the declaration is moved, not the initialization. This can lead to unexpected behavior:

```
console.log(x); // Output: undefined

var x = 10;
```

Here, x is hoisted and declared at the top, but its value is `undefined` until the assignment line is executed.

Potential Issues and Best Practices

Hoisting can cause confusion if you're not aware of it. Variables can appear to have unexpected values, and functions might be called before their definitions are encountered.

To mitigate these issues, consider the following best practices:

- **Declare Variables at the Top:** Declare variables at the beginning of their scope (e.g., the top of a function) to avoid confusion due to hoisting.
- **Use `let` and `const`:** Prefer `let` and `const` for variable declarations, as they have block-level scope and are not hoisted in the same way as `var`.
- **Function Placement:** While function hoisting can be convenient, consider placing function definitions before their usage for clarity.

By understanding the global object and hoisting, you'll gain a deeper appreciation for JavaScript's unique behavior and write code that's more predictable and easier to maintain.

The Infamous `this` Keyword

The `this` keyword in JavaScript is a source of both power and confusion. Unlike other languages where `this` always refers to the current object instance, in JavaScript, its value is determined by the context in which a function is called. This dynamic nature can lead to unexpected results if not understood correctly.

Understanding `this`: It's All About Context

The value of `this` depends on how a function is invoked. There are four main ways `this` can be bound:

1. **Default Binding:** When a function is called standalone, `this` refers to the global object (e.g., `window` in browsers).

   ```
   function sayHello() {
     console.log(this); // In a browser: `window` object
   }
   sayHello();
   ```

2. **Implicit Binding:** When a function is called as a method on an object, `this` refers to that object.

   ```
   const person = {
   ```

```
  name: "Alice",
  greet: function() {
    console.log(this.name); // Output: "Alice"
  }
};
person.greet();
```

3. **Explicit Binding:** You can explicitly set the value of `this` using `call`, `apply`, or `bind`.

```
function sayName(greeting) {
  console.log(greeting + ", " + this.name);
}
const person = { name: "Bob" };

sayName.call(person, "Hello");     // Output: "Hello, Bob"
sayName.apply(person, ["Hi"]);  // Output: "Hi, Bob"

const boundSayName = sayName.bind(person);
boundSayName("Hey");              // Output: "Hey, Bob"
```

4. **New Binding:** When a function is called with the new keyword, a new object is created, and `this` is bound to that new object.

```
function Person(name) {
  this.name = name;
}
const emily = new Person("Emily");
console.log(emily.name); // Output: "Emily"
```

Common Pitfalls and Best Practices

- **Losing `this` in Callbacks:** When passing a function as a callback (e.g., in event listeners or asynchronous operations), the `this` value can be lost. Use `bind`, arrow functions (which lexically inherit `this`), or explicitly pass the context using additional arguments.
- **`this` in Nested Functions:** Nested functions have their own `this` value, which might not be what you expect. Again, arrow functions or explicit binding can help.

```
const obj = {
  outerFunc: function() {
    console.log(this); // obj
    const innerFunc = function() {
      console.log(this); // In a browser: `window` object
    };
    innerFunc();
  }
};

obj.outerFunc();
```

By mastering the different ways `this` can be bound and understanding the common pitfalls, you'll be well-equipped to write clear, predictable, and robust JavaScript code.

The Prototype Chain and Prototypal Inheritance

Prototypes and prototypal inheritance are at the core of JavaScript's object model. Understanding how they work is essential for comprehending object creation, behavior, and relationships.

Prototypes: The Blueprint for Objects

In JavaScript, nearly every object has a special property called `[[Prototype]]`. This property points to another object known as its prototype. Think of the prototype as a blueprint that provides the object with its initial set of properties and methods.

When you access a property or method on an object, JavaScript first checks if the object itself has it. If not, it looks in the object's prototype. If it's still not found, JavaScript continues up the prototype chain, checking each prototype until it reaches the end of the chain.

The Prototype Chain: The Inheritance Trail

The prototype chain is a linked list of objects, starting with the object you're working with and ending with the `Object.prototype`, the root of all objects in JavaScript.

```
const myObject = {};
console.log(myObject.__proto__ === Object.prototype); // Output: true
console.log(Object.prototype.__proto__);              // Output: null
```

The `__proto__` property (or `Object.getPrototypeOf()`) allows you to access an object's prototype directly.

Prototypal Inheritance: Sharing is Caring

Prototypal inheritance is the mechanism by which objects inherit properties and methods from their prototypes. When you create a new object, you can specify its prototype, and it will automatically have access to all the properties and methods of that prototype.

```
const animal = {
  eat() {
    console.log("Yum!");
  }
};

const dog = Object.create(animal); // dog inherits from animal
dog.eat(); // Output: "Yum!"
```

Here, dog inherits the `eat` method from the `animal` object through the prototype chain.

The Importance of Prototypes and Inheritance

Prototypes and inheritance are powerful tools in JavaScript:

- **Code Reuse:** They promote code reusability by allowing objects to share common properties and methods.
- **Dynamic Nature:** You can modify prototypes at runtime, affecting all objects inheriting from them.
- **Foundation of Object Model:** They form the basis of JavaScript's object model, enabling object creation, behavior, and relationships.

Examples in Action

1. **Built-in Objects:** All built-in JavaScript objects inherit from `Object.prototype`. For example, arrays have methods like push, pop, and `forEach`, which are inherited from `Array.prototype`.

2. **Custom Objects:** You can create your own object hierarchies using prototypes. For example, a `Car` object could inherit from a `Vehicle` object, sharing properties like `wheels` and `engine`.

By understanding prototypes, the prototype chain, and prototypal inheritance, you'll gain a deeper appreciation for how JavaScript objects work and how to leverage their power in your code.

Chapter Summary

In this chapter, we explored some of the fundamental "quirks" that make JavaScript unique. We delved into zero-based numbering, the foundation for accessing elements in arrays and strings. We uncovered the potential pitfalls of automatic semicolon insertion and learned how to write more predictable code by embracing explicit semicolons. We also demystified loose typing and type coercion, highlighting the importance of understanding these concepts to prevent unexpected behavior.

Furthermore, we gained insights into the global object, the root of the JavaScript universe, and the concept of hoisting, which influences how variables and functions are accessed. Finally, we embarked on a journey to understand the infamous `this` keyword, its dynamic nature, and the various ways it can be bound.

These concepts might seem quirky at first, but by embracing them and understanding the reasoning behind their design, you'll be well on your way to mastering JavaScript and writing cleaner, more reliable code.

JavaScript's Building Blocks: Variables, Data Types, Operators, and Expressions

Outline

- Variables: The Containers of Your Code
- Data Types: The Essence of Information
- Operators: The Verbs of JavaScript
- Expressions: Putting It All Together
- Chapter Summary

Variables: The Containers of Your Code

Variables are the fundamental building blocks of any JavaScript program. They serve as labeled containers that hold data, allowing you to store, manipulate, and reference information throughout your code. Think of them like boxes with labels, each storing a specific value.

Declaring Variables: `var`, `let`, and `const`

In JavaScript, you have three keywords to declare variables:

- **`var`:** The classic way to declare variables, but its use is generally discouraged in modern JavaScript due to its function-scoped behavior.
- **`let`:** Introduced in ES6 (ECMAScript 2015), `let` declares block-scoped variables, meaning they are only accessible within the specific block of code where they are defined (e.g., within an `if` statement or a loop). You can reassign values to `let` variables.
- **`const`:** Also introduced in ES6, `const` declares block-scoped variables that are constant. This means you cannot reassign a new value to a `const` variable once it has been assigned.

```
var oldWay = 10; // Function-scoped (generally avoid)
let age = 25;      // Block-scoped, can be reassigned
const pi = 3.14;    // Block-scoped, cannot be reassigned
```

Naming Conventions and Best Practices

Choosing meaningful names for your variables is crucial for code readability and maintainability. Here are some guidelines:

- **CamelCase:** Use camelCase for variable names. Start with a lowercase letter and capitalize the first letter of each subsequent word (e.g., `firstName`, `numberOfItems`).
- **Descriptive Names:** Choose names that clearly describe the purpose of the variable. Avoid single-letter variables or cryptic abbreviations.
- **Avoid Reserved Words:** Don't use JavaScript keywords (e.g., `var`, `if`, `function`) as variable names.
- **Be Consistent:** Maintain a consistent naming convention throughout your codebase.

Variable Declaration and Assignment

You declare a variable by using one of the keywords (`var`, `let`, or `const`), followed by the variable name. You can optionally assign an initial value to the variable during declaration.

```
let name;          // Variable declaration
name = "Alice"; // Variable assignment
let age = 30;       // Declaration and assignment in one line

const MAX_ITEMS = 100; // Constant declaration and assignment
```

Key Points to Remember

- **Scope:** Be mindful of variable scope. `var` variables have function scope, while `let` and `const` variables have block scope.
- **Mutability:** Use `const` for values that should not change, `let` for values that might change, and avoid `var` in modern JavaScript.
- **Descriptive Names:** Choose clear and concise names that reflect the purpose of your variables.

By mastering these fundamental concepts, you'll lay a solid foundation for working with variables in JavaScript.

Data Types: The Essence of Information

In the world of JavaScript, data comes in various flavors, each with its own purpose and set of behaviors. Understanding these data types is essential for writing effective code. Let's explore the fundamental data types that underpin JavaScript programming.

Numbers: Counting and Calculating

JavaScript uses a single number type to represent both integers (whole numbers) and floating-point numbers (numbers with decimal points). You can perform arithmetic operations, comparisons, and mathematical calculations with numbers.

```
let age = 30;           // Integer
let price = 9.99;       // Floating-point
let temperature = -5; // Negative number

console.log(age + 10);           // Output: 40
console.log(price * 2);          // Output: 19.98
console.log(Math.abs(temperature)); // Output: 5
```

JavaScript also has special numeric values:

- **`Infinity`:** Represents infinity (positive or negative).
- **NaN (Not a Number):** Indicates an invalid mathematical operation or result.

Strings: Textual Representation

Strings are sequences of characters used to represent text. You can create strings using single quotes ('), double quotes ("), or backticks (`) (template literals).

```
let message = 'Hello, world!';
let greeting = "Greetings!";
let name = `Alice`;

console.log(message.length);            // Output: 13
console.log(greeting.toUpperCase());   // Output: "GREETINGS!"
console.log(`Welcome, ${name}!`);   // Output: "Welcome, Alice!"
```

Strings support various operations like concatenation, finding substrings, and changing case.

Booleans: True or False

Booleans represent logical values: `true` or `false`. They are essential for controlling program flow and making decisions based on conditions.

```
let isStudent = true;
let isRaining = false;

if (isStudent && !isRaining) {
  console.log("Go to school!");
} else {
  console.log("Stay home.");
}
```

Null and Undefined: The Absence of Value

- **`null`:** Represents the intentional absence of a value. It's often used to indicate that a variable has been declared but hasn't been assigned a meaningful value yet.
- **`undefined`:** Indicates a variable that has been declared but has not been assigned any value, or a function that does not return a value.

  ```
  let score = null; // Intentional absence of score
  let result;       // Declared but not assigned, so it's undefined
  ```

Objects: The Key-Value Powerhouses

Objects are collections of key-value pairs. They allow you to group related data and functionality together. Objects are fundamental to JavaScript and are used extensively throughout the language.

```
const person = {
  name: "Bob",
  age: 35,
  sayHello: function() {
    console.log("Hello!");
  }
};

console.log(person.name);   // Output: "Bob"
person.sayHello();         // Output: "Hello!"
```

Symbols: Unique Identifiers

Symbols are a newer data type introduced in ES6. They are used to create unique identifiers for object properties, ensuring that property names won't clash with other properties.

```
const mySymbol = Symbol();
const obj = {
  [mySymbol]: "This is a symbol property"
};
```

Symbols are used in more advanced scenarios, and we won't delve deeply into them in this chapter. By understanding these fundamental data types, you'll be equipped to represent and manipulate various kinds of information in your JavaScript programs. As you progress, you'll discover how these building blocks combine to create complex and powerful applications.

Operators: The Verbs of JavaScript

Operators are the symbols and keywords in JavaScript that perform actions on data. They are the "verbs" of the language, allowing you to manipulate values, compare them, and make decisions based on the results.

Arithmetic Operators: Performing Calculations

These operators perform basic mathematical operations on numeric values:

- **+ (Addition):** Adds two numbers.
- **- (Subtraction):** Subtracts one number from another.
- *** (Multiplication):** Multiplies two numbers.
- **/ (Division):** Divides one number by another.
- **% (Modulo):** Returns the remainder of a division.
- **** (Exponentiation):** Raises a number to the power of another.

```
let x = 10, y = 3;
console.log(x + y);     // Output: 13
console.log(x - y);     // Output: 7
console.log(x * y);     // Output: 30
console.log(x / y);     // Output: 3.3333333333333335
console.log(x % y);     // Output: 1
console.log(2 ** 3);    // Output: 8 (2 to the power of 3)
```

Assignment Operators: Assigning Values

These operators are used to assign values to variables:

- **= (Assignment):** Assigns a value to a variable.
- **+= (Add and Assign):** Adds a value to the existing value of a variable and assigns the result.
- **-= (Subtract and Assign):** Similar to +=, but subtracts instead.
- ***=, /=, %=, **=:** Similar to += and -=, but for multiplication, division, modulo, and exponentiation.

```
let count = 5;
count += 3;   // Equivalent to count = count + 3;  count is now 8
count *= 2;   // Equivalent to count = count * 2;  count is now 16
```

Comparison Operators: Making Comparisons

These operators compare two values and return a boolean (`true` or `false`) result:

- **== (Equality):** Checks if two values are equal(with type coercion).
- **!= (Inequality):** Checks if two values are not equal (with type coercion).
- **> (Greater Than):** Checks if the first value is greater than the second.
- **< (Less Than):** Checks if the first value is less than the second.
- **>= (Greater Than or Equal To):** Checks if the first value is greater than or equal to the second.
- **<= (Less Than or Equal To):** Checks if the first value is less than or equal to the second.

```
console.log(5 == 5);       // Output: true
console.log(5 != '5');     // Output: false (type coercion happens)
console.log(10 > 3);       // Output: true
```

Logical Operators: Combining Conditions

These operators combine boolean expressions:

- **&& (Logical AND):** Returns `true` if both expressions are true.
- **|| (Logical OR):** Returns `true` if at least one expression is true.
- **! (Logical NOT):** Reverses the truthiness of an expression.

```
let isSunny = true;
let isWarm = false;

console.log(isSunny && isWarm); // Output: false
console.log(isSunny || isWarm); // Output: true
console.log(!isSunny);          // Output: false
```

String Operators: Working with Text

- **+ (Concatenation):** Joins two strings together.
- **+= (Concatenation Assignment):** Concatenates a string and assigns the result.

```
let firstName = "John";
let lastName = "Doe";
let fullName = firstName + " " + lastName; // "John Doe"
fullName += ", the JavaScript enthusiast"; // "John Doe, the JavaScript
enthusiast"
```

Other Operators: A Brief Overview

JavaScript has many other operators, including:

- **Ternary Operator (`? :`)**: A shorthand for conditional expressions.
- **`typeof` Operator:** Returns the data type of a value as a string (e.g., "number," "string," "boolean").
- **`delete` Operator:** Deletes a property from an object.

By mastering these operators, you gain the ability to manipulate data, make decisions, and control the flow of your JavaScript programs effectively.

Expressions: Putting It All Together

Expressions are the heart of computation in JavaScript. They are combinations of values, variables, and operators that, when evaluated, produce a result. Think of them as the sentences of your JavaScript code, each expressing a specific action or calculation.

Types of Expressions:

1. **Arithmetic Expressions:** These involve mathematical operations like addition, subtraction, multiplication, and division. They work with numbers and produce numeric results.

```
let sum = 5 + 8; // 13
let product = price * quantity;
```

2. **String Expressions:** These manipulate text (strings). The most common operation is concatenation, which joins strings together.

```
let message = "Hello, " + name + "!";
```

```
let description = `${item.name} costs $${item.price}.`; // Using template
literals
```

3. **Boolean Expressions:** These evaluate to either `true` or `false`. They often use comparison operators (==, !=, >, <, etc.) or logical operators (&&, ||, !).

```
let isEligible = age >= 18 && hasLicense;
let isValidPassword = password.length >= 8;
```

How Expressions are Evaluated

JavaScript evaluates expressions from left to right, following a set of rules called operator precedence and associativity.

- **Operator Precedence:** This determines the order in which operators are applied. For example, multiplication (`*`) and division (`/`) have higher precedence than addition (`+`) and subtraction (`-`).
- **Associativity:** This determines how operators of the same precedence are grouped. Most operators in JavaScript are left-associative, meaning they are evaluated from left to right.

Understanding these rules is crucial for ensuring your expressions are evaluated as you intend.

Using Expressions in JavaScript Code

Expressions are used in many parts of JavaScript code:

- **Assignments:** The right-hand side of an assignment (=) is an expression.
- **Function Arguments:** Expressions are passed as arguments to functions.
- **Return Statements:** Functions often return the result of an expression.
- **Control Structures:** Boolean expressions are used in `if` statements, loops, and other control structures to determine program flow.

Example:

```
function calculateArea(length, width) {
  return length * width; // Arithmetic expression
}

const area = calculateArea(10, 5); // Function call with expressions as
arguments

if (area > 50) { // Boolean expression
  console.log("The area is large.");
} else {
  console.log("The area is small.");
}
```

In this example, the `calculateArea` function takes two arguments (both expressions) and returns the result of multiplying them (another expression). The `if` statement uses a boolean expression to decide which message to print.

Key Takeaway

Mastering expressions is essential for effectively using JavaScript. They form the basis of calculations, decision-making, and data manipulation in your programs. Understanding operator precedence and associativity will help you write code that behaves as you expect, leading to fewer errors and more reliable applications.

Chapter Summary

In this chapter, we delved into the fundamental building blocks of JavaScript. We explored how variables act as containers for storing and manipulating data, emphasizing the importance of choosing appropriate data types like numbers, strings, and booleans to represent different kinds of information. We also discussed how operators function as the “verbs” of the language, allowing us to perform calculations, comparisons, and logical operations. Finally, we learned how expressions combine values, variables, and operators to form the core of computation in JavaScript.

By mastering these concepts, you have laid the groundwork for understanding more complex JavaScript structures and algorithms. You are now equipped to write code that performs calculations, makes decisions, and interacts with data in meaningful ways. As you progress in your JavaScript journey, these building blocks will serve as the foundation upon which you construct more sophisticated applications and programs.

Controlling Flow and Logic: Conditional Statements, Loops, and Functions

Outline

- Conditional Statements: Making Decisions in Your Code
- Loops: Repeating Actions Efficiently
- Functions: Organizing and Reusing Code
- Function Declaration vs. Function Expression
- Chapter Summary

Conditional Statements: Making Decisions in Your Code

Conditional statements are the backbone of logic in programming. They allow your code to make decisions based on specific conditions, choosing different actions to take based on whether a condition is true or false. This ability to branch and adapt based on data is what makes software truly "smart."

`if` Statements: The Fundamental Choice

The `if` statement is the most basic conditional statement. It checks a condition (a boolean expression), and if that condition is true, it executes the code block within its curly braces `{}`.

```
let temperature = 20;

if (temperature > 15) {
  console.log("It's a warm day!");
}
```

In this example, the code inside the `if` block will only execute if `temperature` is greater than 15.

`else` Statements: The Alternative Path

The `else` statement provides an alternative code block to execute if the `if` condition is false.

```
if (temperature > 15) {
  console.log("It's a warm day!");
} else {
  console.log("It's a bit chilly.");
}
```

`else if` Statements: Handling Multiple Conditions

When you need to check multiple conditions in sequence, you can use `else if` statements. Each `else if` block is evaluated only if the preceding `if` and any previous `else if` conditions are false.

```
if (temperature > 25) {
  console.log("It's hot!");
} else if (temperature > 15) {
  console.log("It's warm.");
} else {
  console.log("It's cool.");
```

```
}
```

Real-World Applications

Conditional statements are used extensively in real-world JavaScript applications:

- **User Input Validation:** Checking if user-entered data is valid (e.g., email format, password strength).
- **Form Submission:** Determining if a form should be submitted based on field values.
- **Game Logic:** Controlling game flow based on player actions and game state.
- **Interactive Web Pages:** Modifying page content based on user preferences or device capabilities.

Proper Indentation and Code Organization

Clear and consistent indentation is crucial for making your conditional statements easy to read and understand. Nested `if...else` structures can become complex, so proper indentation helps visualize the logic.

```
// Good indentation
if (condition1) {
  // Code to execute if condition1 is true
} else if (condition2) {
  // Code to execute if condition1 is false and condition2 is true
} else {
  // Code to execute if both condition1 and condition2 are false
}
```

In summary, conditional statements empower your JavaScript code with the ability to make decisions based on various conditions. By mastering `if`, `else if`, and `else`, you'll be able to create more dynamic, interactive, and intelligent applications.

Loops: Repeating Actions Efficiently

Loops are powerful constructs in programming that allow you to automate repetitive tasks. Instead of writing the same code multiple times, you can use a loop to execute a block of code repeatedly as long as a certain condition is met. This saves you time and effort, and it makes your code cleaner and more maintainable.

`for` Loops: The Workhorses of Iteration

The `for` loop is the most common and versatile loop in JavaScript. It consists of three parts:

1. **Initialization:** A variable is initialized to a starting value (e.g., `let i = 0`).
2. **Condition:** A boolean expression is checked before each iteration. The loop continues as long as this condition is true.
3. **Update Expression:** This expression modifies the initialized variable after each iteration (e.g., `i++`).

   ```
   for (let i = 0; i < 5; i++) {
     console.log(i); // Output: 0 1 2 3 4
   }
   ```

   In this example, the loop iterates five times, printing the numbers 0 through 4 to the console.

You can use `for` loops to iterate over arrays and strings:

```
const numbers = [1, 2, 3, 4, 5];
for (let i = 0; i < numbers.length; i++) {
  console.log(numbers[i]);
}

const message = "Hello";
for (let i = 0; i < message.length; i++) {
  console.log(message[i]);
}
```

`while` Loops: Iterate Until a Condition Fails

The `while` loop is simpler than a `for` loop. It executes a block of code repeatedly as long as its condition is true.

```
let count = 0;
while (count < 5) {
  console.log(count);
  count++;
}
```

This loop does the same thing as the `for` loop example above.

`while` loops are often used when the number of iterations is not known in advance, like when waiting for user input or processing data from a stream.

`do...while` Loops: At Least Once, Guaranteed

The `do...while` loop is similar to a `while` loop, but it guarantees that the loop body executes at least once, even if the condition is initially false.

```
let input;
do {
  input = prompt("Enter a number greater than 0:");
} while (input <= 0);
```

This loop will repeatedly prompt the user for input until they enter a number greater than 0.

`for...in` Loops: Iterate Over Object Properties

The `for...in` loop iterates over the enumerable properties of an object. Note that it iterates over property names (keys), not values.

```
const person = { name: "Alice", age: 30, city: "New York" };

for (let key in person) {
  console.log(key + ": " + person[key]);
}
```

This loop will print:

name: Alice
age: 30
city: New York

`for...of` Loops: Iterate Over Iterable Objects

The `for...of` loop is used to iterate over iterable objects like arrays, strings, Maps, Sets, and more. It provides a clean syntax for accessing the values directly.

```
const numbers = [1, 2, 3];
for (let num of numbers) {
  console.log(num);
}
```

Best Practices for Looping

- **Clear Termination Condition:** Ensure your loops have a well-defined condition that will eventually become false to avoid infinite loops.
- **Keep Loop Bodies Concise:** Avoid putting too much logic within the loop body for readability.
- **Choose the Right Loop:** Use the appropriate loop type for the task at hand. `for` loops are generally best for known iteration counts, while `while` and `do...while` loops are better for conditions that may change during iteration.

Loops are an essential tool in your JavaScript arsenal. By understanding the different types of loops and applying best practices, you can write more efficient, maintainable, and expressive code.

Functions: Organizing and Reusing Code

Functions are the backbone of well-structured JavaScript code. They encapsulate blocks of code designed to perform specific tasks, making your programs more organized, efficient, and easier to maintain. Think of functions as self-contained mini-programs that you can call upon whenever you need their specific functionality.

Defining Functions: Two Flavors

There are two primary ways to define functions in JavaScript:

1. **Function Declarations:** The traditional way, using the `function` keyword followed by the function name, parameters in parentheses, and the code block within curly braces.

   ```
   function greet(name) {
     console.log("Hello, " + name + "!");
   }
   ```

2. **Function Expressions (including Arrow Functions):** Assigning a function to a variable. Arrow functions, introduced in ES6, provide a more concise syntax.

   ```
   const greet = function(name) {
     console.log("Hello, " + name + "!");
   };

   // Arrow function syntax (ES6+)
   const greet = (name) => {
     console.log("Hello, " + name + "!");
   };
   ```

Function Parameters and Arguments: Passing Data In

Functions can accept input values called parameters. When you call a function, you provide the actual values known as arguments.

```
function add(a, b) {
  return a + b;
}

let sum = add(5, 3); // 5 and 3 are arguments
console.log(sum);    // Output: 8
```

Return Values: Getting Data Out

Functions can return a value using the `return` statement. This allows you to use the result of a function's computation elsewhere in your code.

```
function square(x) {
  return x * x;
}

let result = square(4);
console.log(result); // Output: 16
```

Calling Functions: Putting Them to Work

You call (execute) a function by using its name followed by parentheses. You can pass arguments inside the parentheses if the function requires them.

```
greet("Alice");        // Output: "Hello, Alice!"
let area = square(5); // Output: 25
```

The Power of Functions

Functions bring several key benefits to your JavaScript code:

- **Reusability:** Write code once and call it multiple times, avoiding repetition.
- **Modularity:** Break down complex tasks into smaller, manageable functions.
- **Organization:** Structure your code into logical blocks, making it easier to read and maintain.
- **Abstraction:** Hide the implementation details of a task, focusing on the desired outcome.

Examples of Functions in Action

- **Calculation:**

  ```
  function calculateTip(billAmount, tipPercentage) {
    return billAmount * (tipPercentage / 100);
  }
  ```

- **Data Manipulation:**

  ```
  function reverseString(str) {
    return str.split('').reverse().join('');
  }
  ```

- **User Interaction:**

  ```
  function askQuestion(question) {
    return prompt(question);
  }
  ```

By mastering functions, you'll unlock the full potential of JavaScript's modularity and reusability, leading to cleaner, more efficient, and more powerful code.

Function Declaration vs. Function Expression

In JavaScript, functions are not just blocks of code; they're also values. This means you can assign functions to variables, pass them as arguments, and return them from other functions. This flexibility leads to two distinct ways of defining functions: function declarations and function expressions.

Function Declarations: The Classic Approach

Function declarations use the `function` keyword, followed by the function name, parameters, and a code block.

```
function sayHello(name) {
  console.log("Hello, " + name + "!");
}
```

Key Characteristics:

- **Hoisting:** Function declarations are hoisted, meaning they are moved to the top of their scope before code execution. This allows you to call a function before it's defined in your code.
- **Named Functions:** Function declarations create named functions, which can be useful for debugging and recursion.

Function Expressions: The Flexible Alternative

Function expressions involve assigning a function to a variable. The function can be named (named function expression) or anonymous (anonymous function expression).

```
const sayGoodbye = function(name) { // Named function expression
  console.log("Goodbye, " + name + "!");
};

const sayFarewell = (name) => {        // Anonymous function expression (arrow
function)
  console.log("Farewell, " + name + "!");
};
```

Key Characteristics:

- **No Hoisting:** Function expressions are not hoisted, so you cannot call them before they are defined in your code.
- **Flexibility:** Function expressions can be passed as arguments to other functions (callbacks) and returned from functions (higher-order functions). This enables powerful functional programming patterns.
- **Anonymous Functions:** Anonymous function expressions are often used when you don't need to refer to the function by name.

Choosing the Right Approach

Both function declarations and function expressions have their place in JavaScript. Here's a quick guideline:

- **Function Declarations:** Use them when you want a simple, straightforward way to define a named function that can be called before it's defined.

- **Function Expressions:** Use them when you need the flexibility to pass functions around as values or when you don't need a named function.

Example: Callbacks and Higher-Order Functions

```
function greet(name, callback) {
  console.log("Greeting:");
  callback(name);
}

greet("Alice", sayHello); // Using a function declaration as a callback
greet("Bob", (name) => { // Using an anonymous function expression as a callback
  console.log("Hi, " + name + "!");
});
```

In this example, the `greet` function takes a callback function as an argument. This demonstrates the flexibility of function expressions and their role in enabling powerful programming techniques like callbacks and higher-order functions.

Chapter Summary

In this chapter, we explored the essential tools for controlling flow and logic in JavaScript. We learned how to use conditional statements (`if`, `else if`, and `else`) to make decisions based on varying conditions, enabling our code to branch and adapt. We then delved into the power of loops (`for`, `while`, `do...while`, `for...in`, and `for...of`) for automating repetitive tasks and iterating over data structures like arrays and objects. Finally, we discovered the importance of functions in organizing, reusing, and modularizing code, and we explored the differences between function declarations and function expressions, unlocking the flexibility of callbacks and higher-order functions.

With these tools in your JavaScript toolbox, you're now equipped to write code that can intelligently respond to different scenarios, efficiently process large amounts of data, and maintain a well-structured and organized codebase. These concepts form a crucial foundation for building more complex applications and understanding advanced JavaScript patterns and techniques.

Mastering the `this` Keyword: Context, Binding, and Common Pitfalls

Outline

- Understanding the Dynamic Nature of `this`
- The Four Binding Rules of `this`
- Common Pitfalls with `this`
- Best Practices for Mastering `this`
- Chapter Summary

Understanding the Dynamic Nature of `this`

In most programming languages, the keyword `this` has a straightforward meaning: it refers to the instance of the object whose method is being called. For example, in a class-based language like Java, `this` always points to the current object within which the method is defined.

JavaScript, however, takes a different approach. The `this` keyword in JavaScript is a dynamic chameleon. Its value doesn't depend on where a function is defined, but rather on how it's called. This means `this` can refer to different objects depending on the context of the function invocation.

Think of `this` as a placeholder that gets filled in with the appropriate object at runtime, based on the way the function is called. This dynamic nature can be a source of confusion, especially for developers coming from other languages where `this` has a more static behavior.

Why Does JavaScript's `this` Behave This Way?

The design choice behind JavaScript's dynamic `this` stems from the language's flexibility and its support for various programming paradigms. It allows functions to be used in different ways:

- **As methods on objects:** In this case, `this` refers to the object.
- **As standalone functions:** Here, `this` refers to the global object (usually `window` in web browsers).
- **As constructor functions:** When used with the `new` keyword, `this` refers to the newly created object.
- **With explicit binding:** You can explicitly set the value of `this` using methods like `call`, `apply`, or `bind`.

This flexibility allows JavaScript functions to be more reusable and adaptable to different scenarios. However, it also means that you need to be mindful of the calling context to understand what `this` refers to at any given time.

Why Understanding `this` Matters

Mastering the behavior of `this` is crucial for several reasons:

- **Avoiding Errors:** Incorrect assumptions about `this` can lead to bugs and unexpected behavior in your code.

- **Writing Reusable Code:** Understanding how `this` works enables you to write functions that can be used in various contexts without unexpected side effects.
- **Leveraging Advanced Features:** Features like object-oriented programming and functional programming in JavaScript heavily rely on the proper use of `this`.

By understanding the dynamic nature of `this`, you'll gain a deeper appreciation for JavaScript's flexibility and be better equipped to write robust, reusable, and elegant code.

The Four Binding Rules of `this`

JavaScript provides four distinct ways to bind the `this` keyword within a function, each with its own rules and implications. Let's explore these binding mechanisms:

1. Default Binding: Standalone Functions

When a function is called without any explicit context (i.e., not as a method on an object), `this` defaults to the global object. In a browser, this usually means the `window` object.

```
function sayHi() {
    console.log(this); // Refers to the global object (window)
    console.log(this === window); // Output: true (in a browser)
}

sayHi();
```

Nested Functions and Default Binding:

Even within nested functions, `this` still defaults to the global object unless another binding rule applies.

```
function outerFunction() {
    function innerFunction() {
        console.log(this); // Refers to the global object (window)
    }
    innerFunction();
}

outerFunction();
```

2. Implicit Binding: Object Methods

When a function is called as a method on an object, `this` is implicitly bound to that object.

```
const person = {
    name: "Alice",
    greet() {
        console.log("Hello, " + this.name + "!");
    }
};

person.greet(); // Output: "Hello, Alice!" (this refers to the person object)
```

3. Explicit Binding: `call`, `apply`, and `bind`

JavaScript provides methods to explicitly set the value of `this` when calling a function:

- **`call`:** Immediately calls the function, passing the `this` value as the first argument, followed by the function's arguments.
- **`apply`:** Similar to `call`, but accepts the function's arguments as an array.
- **`bind`:** Returns a new function with `this` permanently bound to the specified value.

```
function greet(greeting) {
    console.log(greeting + ", " + this.name + "!");
}

const person1 = { name: "Bob" };
const person2 = { name: "Charlie" };

greet.call(person1, "Hello");    // Output: "Hello, Bob!"
greet.apply(person2, ["Hi"]);   // Output: "Hi, Charlie!"

const boundGreet = greet.bind(person1);
boundGreet("Hey");              // Output: "Hey, Bob!"
```

4. New Binding: Constructor Functions

When a function is called with the new keyword, a new object is created, and `this` is bound to this newly created object. Functions called with new are often referred to as constructor functions.

```
function Person(name) {
    this.name = name;
}

const david = new Person("David");
console.log(david.name); // Output: "David"
```

By understanding these four binding rules, you can predict and control the behavior of `this` in your JavaScript code, making it a valuable tool rather than a source of confusion.

Common Pitfalls with `this`

While `this` can be a powerful tool, it's also prone to causing confusion and errors if you're not careful. Let's explore two common scenarios where `this` can behave unexpectedly:

Losing `this` in Callbacks

Callbacks are functions passed as arguments to other functions and are often used in event handlers and asynchronous operations. The problem is that when a callback function is executed, it might not have the same `this` context as the function it was defined within.

```
const myObject = {
    name: "MyObject",
    logName: function() {
        console.log(this.name);
    }
};

setTimeout(myObject.logName, 1000); // Output: undefined
```

In this example, `setTimeout` calls the `logName` method after a delay, but by that time, `this` within `logName` refers to the global object (window), not `myObject`.

Solutions: Preserving `this` in Callbacks

1. **Using `bind`:**

   ```
   setTimeout(myObject.logName.bind(myObject), 1000); // Output: "MyObject"
   ```

   The `bind` method creates a new function with `this` permanently bound to the specified object.

2. **Arrow Functions:**

   ```
   const myObject = {
       name: "MyObject",
       logName: () => {  // Arrow function
           console.log(this.name);
       }
   };

   setTimeout(myObject.logName, 1000); // Output: "MyObject"
   ```

   Arrow functions lexically bind `this`, meaning they inherit the `this` value from the surrounding scope where they are defined.

3. **Closures:**

   ```
   const myObject = {
       name: "MyObject",
       logName: function() {
           const self = this; // Save reference to 'this'
           setTimeout(function() {
               console.log(self.name); // Use 'self'
           }, 1000);
       }
   };

   myObject.logName(); // Output: "MyObject"
   ```

   By creating a closure, you can capture the value of `this` in a variable (`self`) and use it within the callback.

Nested Functions and `this`

When a function is nested inside another function, the inner function has its own `this` context. This can lead to confusion if you expect the inner function to inherit the `this` value from the outer function.

```
const myObject = {
    name: "MyObject",
    outerFunc: function() {
        console.log(this.name); // Output: "MyObject"

        function innerFunc() {
            console.log(this.name); // Output: undefined
        }
        innerFunc();
```

```
    }
};

myObject.outerFunc();
```

Solutions: Managing `this` in Nested Functions

1. **Arrow Functions:**

```
innerFunc = () => { // Arrow function
    console.log(this.name); // Output: "MyObject"
};
```

2. **Closures:**

```
const self = this;
function innerFunc() {
    console.log(self.name); // Output: "MyObject"
}
```

In both solutions, the inner function accesses the `this` value from the outer function's scope.

By being aware of these common pitfalls and applying the appropriate solutions, you can ensure that the `this` keyword works as expected in your JavaScript code.

Best Practices for Mastering `this`

To confidently wield the power of `this`, adopt these best practices:

1. Understand Context, Always

The golden rule of `this` is to always be aware of the context in which a function is called. Ask yourself:

- **Is it a standalone function?** If so, `this` will likely be the global object.
- **Is it a method on an object?** Then `this` will usually be that object.
- **Is it a callback?** Be cautious, as `this` might be lost or point to the global object.
- **Is it called with new?** In a constructor, `this` refers to the newly created object.

By analyzing the context, you can predict and control `this` behavior.

2. Explicit Binding: Precision Control

When you need precise control over the `this` value, don't hesitate to use explicit binding methods:

- **`call`:** Useful for immediate function calls with individual arguments.
- **`apply`:** Handy when you have arguments in an array.
- **`bind`:** Creates a new function with a pre-set `this` value, ideal for passing functions around.

```
const person = { name: "Alice" };

function greet(message) {
    console.log(message + ", " + this.name + "!");
}
```

```
greet.call(person, "Hello");          // Output: "Hello, Alice!"
greet.apply(person, ["Greetings"]);   // Output: "Greetings, Alice!"

const boundGreet = greet.bind(person);
boundGreet("Hi");                     // Output: "Hi, Alice!"
```

3. Arrow Functions for Callbacks

Arrow functions offer a streamlined way to handle callbacks, as they automatically inherit the `this` value from their surrounding scope (lexical `this`).

```
const myObject = {
    name: "MyObject",
    logName: () => {  // Arrow function
        console.log(this.name);
    }
};

setTimeout(myObject.logName, 1000); // Output: "MyObject"
```

This eliminates the need for manual binding in most callback scenarios.

4. Constructor Functions with new: Object Creation

When creating objects with the `new` keyword, the function (constructor) automatically sets `this` to the newly created object.

```
function Car(brand) {
    this.brand = brand;
}

const myCar = new Car("Toyota");
console.log(myCar.brand); // Output: "Toyota"
```

Practice Makes Perfect

The best way to master `this` is through hands-on practice. Experiment with different binding scenarios, use the techniques we've discussed, and observe how `this` behaves in various contexts. By putting these concepts into action, you'll gain the confidence and expertise needed to harness the full power of `this` in your JavaScript code.

Chapter Summary

In this chapter, we've embarked on a journey to tame the elusive `this` keyword in JavaScript. We started by understanding its dynamic nature and how its value is determined by the context of the function call. We then explored the four binding rules that govern `this`: default binding, implicit binding, explicit binding, and new binding. Along the way, we uncovered common pitfalls that can lead to errors, such as losing `this` in callbacks and nested functions.

By now, you should have a firm grasp of how `this` works in different scenarios and the strategies you can use to control its behavior. Remember, mastering `this` requires understanding the context of the function call and choosing the appropriate binding method. With practice and a keen eye for context, you'll be able to confidently wield this powerful yet quirky feature of JavaScript to write clearer, more reliable, and more flexible code.

Section II:

Objects: The Heart of JavaScript

Object Essentials: Creating, Accessing, and Manipulating Objects

Outline

- Understanding Objects in JavaScript
- Creating Objects
- Accessing Object Properties
- Modifying Objects
- Common Object Methods
- Chapter Summary

Understanding Objects in JavaScript

Objects are the very heart of JavaScript. They are the primary way to represent structured data and the foundation for building complex applications. In essence, objects are collections of key-value pairs. Each key is a string (or, less commonly, a symbol), and each value can be anything: a number, a string, a boolean, another object, or even a function.

Imagine an object as a container with labeled compartments. Each compartment has a label (the key) and something stored inside (the value). You can use these labels to access and manipulate the contents of each compartment.

Objects as Real-World Models

Objects are particularly powerful because they allow you to model real-world entities and concepts within your code. For example, consider a `person` object:

```
const person = {
  firstName: "John",
  lastName: "Doe",
  age: 30,
  occupation: "Engineer",
  hobbies: ["reading", "coding", "hiking"]
};
```

This object represents a person with various attributes like name, age, occupation, and hobbies. Each attribute is a key-value pair. The keys are strings like “firstName,” “lastName,” etc., and the values are the corresponding data associated with each attribute.

Beyond Simple Data: Objects and Functionality

Objects can also contain functions, which are known as methods in the context of objects. Methods allow objects to perform actions or exhibit behavior.

```
const car = {
  brand: "Toyota",
  model: "Camry",
  startEngine() {
    console.log("Engine started!");
  },
  accelerate() {
    console.log("Vroom!");
  }
};
```

In this example, the `car` object has methods like `startEngine()` and `accelerate()`, which represent actions the car can take.

Objects and Complex Data Structures

Objects are not limited to representing simple entities. You can use them to create complex data structures by nesting objects within objects. For instance, you could have an object representing a `library` that contains an array of book objects, each with its own properties like `title`, `author`, and `genre`.

```
const library = {
  name: "City Library",
  address: "123 Main Street",
  books: [
    { title: "The Hitchhiker's Guide to the Galaxy", author: "Douglas Adams"
},
    { title: "Pride and Prejudice", author: "Jane Austen" }
    // ...more books
  ]
};
```

In this way, objects provide a flexible and intuitive way to organize and structure data in JavaScript. They are a cornerstone of the language, used for everything from simple data storage to creating complex applications and frameworks. By mastering objects, you'll unlock a world of possibilities for building sophisticated JavaScript programs.

Creating Objects

The different ways to create objects in JavaScript:

1. Object Literal Notation:

Object literal notation is the simplest and most common way to create objects in JavaScript. It's a concise and intuitive way to define an object's structure directly in your code.

Syntax: Curly Braces and Key-Value Pairs

The syntax for object literals is straightforward:

```
const myObject = {
    key1: value1,
    key2: value2,
    // ...more key-value pairs
};
```

The object is enclosed within curly braces {}. Inside the braces, you define key-value pairs, separated by commas. Each key-value pair represents a property of the object:

- **Key:** A string (or symbol) that acts as the property name.
- **Value:** The data associated with the property. Values can be of any data type, including numbers, strings, booleans, arrays, functions, or even other objects.

Examples: Bringing Objects to Life

Let's create some objects using object literal notation:

```
// Simple object with properties
const person = {
    firstName: "Alice",
    lastName: "Johnson",
    age: 30
};

// Object with properties and a method
const dog = {
    name: "Max",
    breed: "Golden Retriever",
    bark: function() {
        console.log("Woof!");
    }
};

// Object with nested objects
const student = {
    name: "Emily",
    grades: {
        math: 90,
        science: 85,
        english: 92
    }
};
```

In the `person` object, we have properties representing the person's first name, last name, and age. The `dog` object has properties for name and breed, as well as a `bark` method that logs "Woof!" to the console when called. Finally, the `student` object demonstrates how you can nest objects within objects to represent more complex structures.

Accessing and Using Object Properties

Once you've created an object, you can access its properties using either dot notation or bracket notation:

```
console.log(person.firstName);          // Output: "Alice"
console.log(dog["breed"]);             // Output: "Golden Retriever"
console.log(student.grades.math);        // Output: 90
dog.bark();                          // Output: "Woof!"
```

Object literal notation is a fundamental tool for creating objects in JavaScript. Its simplicity and flexibility make it ideal for representing a wide range of data and structures.

2. Constructor Functions:

Constructor functions offer a blueprint-like approach to object creation in JavaScript. They define a template for objects, allowing you to create multiple instances of objects with the same structure and initial properties.

Defining Constructor Functions

A constructor function is a regular JavaScript function with a few conventions:

1. **Naming:** Constructor function names are conventionally capitalized (e.g., `Person`, `Car`, `Book`). This helps distinguish them from regular functions.
2. **`this` Keyword:** Inside the constructor, the `this` keyword refers to the newly created object instance. You use `this` to assign properties and methods to the object.

```
function Person(firstName, lastName, age) {
    this.firstName = firstName;
    this.lastName = lastName;
    this.age = age;
    this.greet = function() {
        console.log(`Hello, my name is ${this.firstName}
${this.lastName}.`);
    };
}
```

In this example, `Person` is a constructor function that takes three parameters (`firstName`, `lastName`, and `age`). It uses `this` to assign these values as properties of the new object. It also defines a `greet` method that logs a greeting message.

Creating Object Instances with new

To create an object instance from a constructor function, you use the `new` keyword:

```
const john = new Person("John", "Doe", 30);
const jane = new Person("Jane", "Smith", 25);
```

Here, `john` and `jane` are two separate instances of the `Person` object, each with its own set of properties and the `greet` method. You can access their properties and call their methods using dot notation:

```
console.log(john.firstName); // Output: "John"
john.greet();                // Output: "Hello, my name is John Doe."

console.log(jane.lastName);  // Output: "Smith"
jane.greet();                // Output: "Hello, my name is Jane Smith."
```

Advantages of Constructor Functions

- **Code Reusability:** Constructor functions avoid repetitive code for creating similar objects.
- **Customizable Initialization:** You can pass arguments to the constructor function to customize the initial state of each object instance.
- **Methods:** You can define methods within the constructor function, giving each object instance its own behavior.

Constructor functions are a powerful tool for creating objects in JavaScript. They offer a structured way to define object templates and instantiate multiple objects with similar properties and behaviors.

3. Object.create() Method:

While constructor functions are a common way to create objects, JavaScript offers a more direct way to control inheritance through the `Object.create()` method. This method allows you to explicitly specify the prototype of a new object, giving you greater control over the inheritance chain.

Understanding `Object.create()`

The `Object.create()` method takes two arguments:

1. **`prototype` (Required):** The object that should serve as the prototype for the newly created object.
2. **`propertiesObject` (Optional):** An object that defines additional properties to add to the new object.

    ```
    const animal = {
      eat() {
        console.log("Yum!");
      }
    };

    const dog = Object.create(animal);
    ```

    In this example, dog is created with `animal` as its prototype. This means `dog` will inherit the `eat()` method from `animal`.

Prototypal Inheritance with `Object.create()`

`Object.create()` provides a clear way to establish inheritance relationships between objects. The new object inherits properties and methods from its specified prototype, forming a prototype chain.

```
console.log(dog.eat);       // Output: ƒ eat() { console.log("Yum!"); }
dog.eat();                  // Output: "Yum!"
```

You can also add properties to the newly created object using the second argument:

```
const myDog = Object.create(animal, {
  name: { value: "Fido" },
  breed: { value: "Golden Retriever" }
});
```

Advantages of `Object.create()`

- **Explicit Prototypal Inheritance:** `Object.create()` makes the inheritance relationship explicit, leading to more readable code.
- **Flexible Prototypes:** You can use any object as the prototype, not just constructor functions. This allows for greater flexibility in designing object hierarchies.
- **No Automatic Properties:** Unlike constructor functions, `Object.create()` doesn't add any extra properties to the new object (like the `constructor` property).

Use Cases for `Object.create()`

- **Pure Prototypal Inheritance:** When you want to create objects without the need for constructor functions.
- **Custom Object Creation:** When you need fine-grained control over the prototype of a new object.
- **Performance Optimization:** In some cases, `Object.create()` can be more efficient than using constructor functions, especially when dealing with large object hierarchies.

By leveraging `Object.create()`, you can create objects that inherit properties and behaviors from other objects in a more explicit and controlled manner. This method provides a valuable alternative to constructor functions for building object-oriented structures in JavaScript.

4. Class Syntax (ES6+):

In modern JavaScript (ES6 and later), you can use class syntax to define objects. While classes provide a more familiar structure for developers coming from object-oriented languages, it's important to understand that they are essentially "syntactic sugar" over the prototypal inheritance model we've already discussed.

Introducing Classes

Classes offer a cleaner and more organized way to define objects and their behaviors. They use the `class` keyword, followed by the class name, curly braces `{}`, and the class body.

```
class Person {
  constructor(firstName, lastName, age) {
    this.firstName = firstName;
    this.lastName = lastName;
    this.age = age;
  }

  greet() {
    console.log(`Hello, my name is ${this.firstName} ${this.lastName}.`);
  }
}
```

In this example, `Person` is a class. The `constructor` method initializes the object's properties when a new instance is created. The `greet` method is a function attached to the class prototype, which all instances of `Person` will inherit.

Creating Instances with the `new` Keyword

To create objects from a class, you use the new keyword, just like with constructor functions:

```
const alice = new Person("Alice", "Johnson", 30);
alice.greet(); // Output: "Hello, my name is Alice Johnson."
```

Syntactic Sugar, Not a New Paradigm

It's important to remember that classes in JavaScript don't fundamentally change how objects work under the hood. They are a more convenient syntax for working with prototypes and constructor functions. Underneath, the same prototypal inheritance mechanism is at play.

Deeper Dive in Later Chapters

In later chapters, we'll explore classes in more depth, covering topics like inheritance, static methods, and advanced class patterns. For now, consider class syntax as a cleaner and more structured way to define objects, but keep in mind that it's built upon the fundamental principles of prototypes and inheritance.

Accessing Object Properties

Once you've created an object, you need to know how to retrieve the data stored within its properties. JavaScript offers two primary ways to access object properties: dot notation and bracket notation.

1. Dot Notation: The Straightforward Approach

Dot notation is the most common and intuitive way to access object properties. It uses a dot (`.`) followed by the property name.

```
const person = {
  name: "Alice",
  age: 30
};

console.log(person.name); // Output: "Alice"
console.log(person.age);  // Output: 30
```

Dot notation is concise and easy to read, making it ideal for accessing properties with simple, predictable names.

2. Bracket Notation: The Flexible Powerhouse

Bracket notation provides a more dynamic way to access properties. Instead of directly writing the property name after the dot, you enclose the property name in square brackets ([ ]).

```
console.log(person["name"]); // Output: "Alice"
```

The real power of bracket notation comes when you use variables to access properties dynamically:

```
const propertyName = "age";
console.log(person[propertyName]); // Output: 30
```

Accessing Nested Properties

Bracket notation is also essential for accessing properties of nested objects.

```
const student = {
  name: "Bob",
  grades: {
    math: 90,
    science: 85
  }
};

console.log(student["grades"]["math"]); // Output: 90
```

When to Use Which Notation

- **Dot Notation:** Prefer dot notation when you know the property name in advance and it's a valid JavaScript identifier (doesn't contain spaces or special characters).
- **Bracket Notation:** Use bracket notation when:
    - You need to use variables to access property names dynamically.
    - The property name is not a valid JavaScript identifier (e.g., contains spaces).
    - You're accessing nested properties.

Choosing the Right Tool

Both dot notation and bracket notation are valuable tools in your JavaScript arsenal. By understanding their strengths and weaknesses, you can choose the most appropriate method for accessing object properties in different situations.

Modifying Objects

Objects in JavaScript are not static entities. You can dynamically add new properties, change existing values, or even remove properties as needed. This flexibility allows your code to adapt and evolve as your application runs.

1. Adding Properties: Expanding the Object

You can easily add new properties to an object after it's been created. Both dot notation and bracket notation work for this purpose.

```
const person = {
  name: "Alice",
  age: 30
};

// Adding a property using dot notation
person.city = "New York";

// Adding a property using bracket notation
person["occupation"] = "Engineer";

console.log(person);
// Output: { name: "Alice", age: 30, city: "New York", occupation: "Engineer"
}
```

2. Modifying Property Values: Updating the Data

To change the value of an existing property, simply assign a new value to it using dot or bracket notation.

```
person.age = 31;            // Update age using dot notation
person["city"] = "San Francisco"; // Update city using bracket notation
```

3. Deleting Properties: Removing What's No Longer Needed

The `delete` operator removes a property from an object.

```
delete person.occupation;
console.log(person);
// Output: { name: "Alice", age: 31, city: "San Francisco" }
```

When to Modify Objects

You might need to modify objects in various scenarios:

- **User Interaction:** Updating user profile information or preferences.
- **Data Updates:** Incorporating new data from an API or database.
- **State Management:** Changing the state of your application in response to events.
- **Dynamic Configurations:** Adjusting settings or options based on user input or other conditions.

Cautions and Considerations

- **Immutability:** In some cases, it's desirable to keep objects immutable (unchangeable). You can use techniques like `Object.freeze()` to prevent modifications.
- **Property Existence:** Before modifying or deleting a property, it's a good practice to check if it exists to avoid errors.

Modifying objects is a fundamental aspect of JavaScript development. By mastering these techniques, you'll be able to create more dynamic and adaptable applications that can respond to changing data and user interactions.

Common Object Methods

JavaScript provides several built-in methods that make working with objects easier and more efficient. Let's explore some of the most essential ones:

`Object.keys(obj)`: Get All the Keys

This method returns an array containing the names (keys) of all the enumerable properties of the given object.

```
const person = {
  name: "Alice",
  age: 30,
  city: "New York"
};

const keys = Object.keys(person);
console.log(keys); // Output: ["name", "age", "city"]
```

`Object.values(obj)`: Get All the Values

This method returns an array containing the values of all the enumerable properties of the given object.

```
const values = Object.values(person);
console.log(values); // Output: ["Alice", 30, "New York"]
```

`Object.entries(obj)`: Get Key-Value Pairs

This method returns an array of arrays, where each inner array represents a key-value pair of the object.

```
const entries = Object.entries(person);
console.log(entries);
// Output: [["name", "Alice"], ["age", 30], ["city", "New York"]]
```

`Object.assign(target, ...sources)`: Copy Properties

This method is used to copy the values of all enumerable own properties from one or more source objects to a target object. It returns the target object.

```
const target = { a: 1 };
const source1 = { b: 2 };
const source2 = { c: 3 };

Object.assign(target, source1, source2);
console.log(target); // Output: { a: 1, b: 2, c: 3 }
```

`Object.freeze(obj)`: Make Objects Immutable

This method freezes an object, preventing new properties from being added to it, existing properties from being removed, and preventing the values of existing properties from being changed. In essence, it makes the object immutable.

```
const person = {
  name: "Alice",
  age: 30
};

Object.freeze(person);

person.age = 31; // This will have no effect
delete person.name; // This will have no effect
```

Why These Methods Are Essential

- **Iteration:** `Object.keys()`, `Object.values()`, and `Object.entries()` are essential for iterating over object properties.
- **Data Manipulation:** `Object.assign()` provides a convenient way to copy or merge objects.
- **State Management:** `Object.freeze()` can be used to enforce immutability in state management libraries (like Redux).

By mastering these common object methods, you'll be equipped with a powerful toolkit to handle objects effectively in your JavaScript applications.

Chapter Summary

In this chapter, we explored the essential concepts of working with objects in JavaScript. We learned that objects are collections of key-value pairs, serving as the foundation for representing structured data and complex entities within your code.

We covered various techniques for creating objects, including object literal notation, constructor functions, and the `Object.create()` method. Each method offers its own advantages and use cases, giving you flexibility in how you construct objects. We also learned how to access and modify object properties using dot notation and bracket notation, providing the ability to dynamically interact with object data.

Finally, we explored some common object methods like `Object.keys()`, `Object.values()`, `Object.entries()`, `Object.assign()`, and `Object.freeze()`. These methods empower you to iterate over properties, copy or merge objects, and even enforce immutability when needed.

With this knowledge, you're well on your way to becoming proficient in working with objects, a fundamental aspect of JavaScript programming. As you continue your journey, you'll discover how objects form the backbone of many JavaScript libraries, frameworks, and applications.

Prototypes and Inheritance: The Prototype Chain and Object Relationships

Outline

- Prototypes: The Underlying Blueprint
- The Prototype Chain: The Inheritance Trail
- Prototypal Inheritance in Action
- `__proto__` vs. `prototype`: Clearing the Confusion
- The Power and Flexibility of Prototypal Inheritance
- Chapter Summary

Prototypes: The Underlying Blueprint

At the core of JavaScript's object model lies the concept of prototypes. Think of a prototype as an object's genetic blueprint, a template that defines its inherited characteristics. Every object in JavaScript, except for `null`, has a hidden link to another object—its prototype.

The Prototype Connection

This hidden link, often referred to as the `[[Prototype]]` property or the `__proto__` property (for legacy reasons), establishes a chain of inheritance. When you try to access a property or method on an object, JavaScript first checks if the object itself possesses that property or method. If not, it follows the `[[Prototype]]` link to the object's prototype and looks for it there. If it's still not found, JavaScript continues up the chain, examining each prototype's prototype, until it reaches the end of the line.

Inherited Traits: The Power of Prototypes

This prototype chain is the mechanism through which JavaScript objects inherit properties and methods. If an object doesn't have a property or method defined directly on it, JavaScript will automatically look for it in the object's prototype. If found, the object can use that inherited property or method as if it were its own. This enables a powerful form of code reuse and dynamic object behavior.

```
const animal = {
  breathe: function() {
    console.log("Inhale and exhale...");
  }
};

const dog = Object.create(animal); // Create 'dog' with 'animal' as its prototype

dog.breathe();  // Output: "Inhale and exhale..."
```

In this example, the dog object doesn't have a `breathe` method defined directly on it. However, because its prototype is the `animal` object, it can access and call the `breathe` method as if it were its own.

The Base of It All: `Object.prototype`

The prototype chain doesn't stretch on forever. At the top of the chain is the `Object.prototype` object. It's the ancestral prototype from which all other objects in JavaScript inherit fundamental properties and methods like `toString()` and `hasOwnProperty()`. This means that even if you create an empty object literal (`{}`), it still implicitly inherits from `Object.prototype`.

Beyond Inheritance: Dynamic Behavior

Prototypes aren't just about inheritance; they also enable dynamic behavior. You can modify a prototype object at runtime, and those changes will be reflected in all objects inheriting from it. This flexibility allows you to create dynamic object relationships and change an object's behavior on the fly.

Understanding prototypes is crucial for grasping how JavaScript objects work. They are the backbone of JavaScript's object model, enabling inheritance, code reuse, and dynamic behavior. By mastering this concept, you'll be well on your way to unlocking the full potential of objects in your JavaScript programs.

The Prototype Chain: The Inheritance Trail

Think of the prototype chain as a family tree of objects, where each object inherits traits (properties and methods) from its ancestors. When you try to access something on an object, JavaScript starts by looking directly at that object. If it can't find what you're looking for, it doesn't give up; it follows a path up the family tree, checking each ancestor in turn.

Visualizing the Chain

```
Object.prototype
    ↑
  Animal.prototype
    ↑
    Dog.prototype
    ↑
    myDog
```

In this diagram:

- **`myDog`:** Your specific dog object (e.g., a Golden Retriever named Max).
- **`Dog.prototype`:** The prototype for all dogs, containing shared dog-like characteristics (e.g., a `bark` method).
- **`Animal.prototype`:** The prototype for all animals, containing even more general traits (e.g., an `eat` method).
- **`Object.prototype`:** The root of all objects, providing basic methods like `toString()`.

The Search Process

Let's say you try to call `myDog.bark()`. Here's how JavaScript finds the method:

1. **Check `myDog`:** Does myDog have a `bark` method directly defined? If yes, call it and stop.
2. **Check `Dog.prototype`:** Does the prototype for dogs have a `bark` method? If yes, call it and stop.
3. **Check `Animal.prototype`:** Does the prototype for animals have a `bark` method? If yes, call it and stop.
4. **Check `Object.prototype`:** Does the base prototype have a `bark` method? If yes, call it.
5. **Not Found:** If the method isn't found anywhere in the chain, JavaScript throws an error.

Code Example

```
const animal = {
  eat() { console.log("Yum!"); }
```

```
};

const dog = Object.create(animal);
dog.bark = function() { console.log("Woof!"); };

dog.eat();     // Output: "Yum!" (inherited from animal)
dog.bark();    // Output: "Woof!" (directly on the dog object)
dog.sleep(); // Error: dog.sleep is not a function (not found in prototype
chain)
```

Key Points

- **Efficiency:** The prototype chain allows for efficient memory use. Objects only store properties unique to them, not the ones they inherit.
- **Flexibility:** You can modify prototypes at runtime, dynamically altering the behavior of objects.
- **The `Object.prototype`:** Every object ultimately inherits from `Object.prototype`, granting access to universal methods.
- **Order Matters:** JavaScript searches the prototype chain from the bottom up, starting with the object itself.

Prototypal Inheritance in Action

Prototypal inheritance is the mechanism that makes JavaScript's object model tick. It allows you to create objects that inherit characteristics from other objects, forming a hierarchical structure.

`Object.create()`: The Inheritance Tool

The `Object.create()` method is the key to creating objects with explicit prototypes. Let's see it in action:

```
// Parent Prototype
const vehicle = {
  startEngine() {
    console.log("Engine starting...");
  }
};

// Child Object
const car = Object.create(vehicle);
car.brand = "Toyota";
car.model = "Camry";
car.drive = function() {
    console.log("Driving...");
}

car.startEngine(); // Output: "Engine starting..." (Inherited from vehicle)
console.log(car.brand); // Output: "Toyota" (Direct property on car)
car.drive(); // Output: "Driving..." (Direct method on car)
```

In this example:

1. We create a `vehicle` object with the `startEngine` method.
2. We use `Object.create(vehicle)` to create a `car` object that inherits from `vehicle`.
3. The `car` object has its own properties (`brand` and `model`) and a method (`drive`).

4. When we call `car.startEngine()`, it's not found on the `car` object itself, so JavaScript looks up the prototype chain to `vehicle`, where it finds and executes the method.

Dynamic Prototypes: Changing the Inheritance

One of the most powerful aspects of prototypal inheritance is that you can modify prototypes at runtime. This change affects all objects inheriting from that prototype.

```
vehicle.startEngine = function() {
  console.log("Engine starting with a roar!"); // Modified method
};

car.startEngine(); // Output: "Engine starting with a roar!"
```

Even though we didn't change the `car` object directly, it now inherits the modified `startEngine` method from its prototype.

The Flexibility of `Object.create()`

Unlike constructor functions, where the prototype is fixed at the time of function definition, `Object.create()` allows you to choose the prototype dynamically. This gives you finer control over inheritance relationships and lets you create complex object hierarchies.

Key Takeaways

- Prototypal inheritance allows objects to share properties and methods through a prototype chain.
- `Object.create()` is a powerful tool for establishing explicit inheritance relationships.
- Modifying a prototype affects all objects inheriting from it.

By understanding prototypal inheritance, you gain a deeper understanding of JavaScript's object model and can create more flexible, reusable, and efficient code.

`__proto__` vs. `prototype`: Clearing the Confusion

The terms `__proto__` and `prototype` are often used interchangeably, leading to confusion about their roles in JavaScript's prototypal inheritance. Let's clarify their distinct purposes and how they work together.

`__proto__`: The Hidden Link

- **Nature:** The `__proto__` property (or its modern equivalent, `Object.getPrototypeOf()`) is an accessor property present on almost all objects in JavaScript.
- **Role:** It serves as a hidden link that points to the object's prototype. This link forms the foundation of the prototype chain, enabling inheritance.
- **Usage:** You can use `__proto__` (or `Object.getPrototypeOf()`) to inspect or even modify an object's prototype. However, direct manipulation of `__proto__` is generally discouraged due to potential performance issues and compatibility concerns.

  ```
  const animal = { eats: true };
  const rabbit = Object.create(animal);

  console.log(rabbit.__proto__ === animal);  // Output: true
  console.log(Object.getPrototypeOf(rabbit) === animal); // Output: true
  ```

`prototype`: The Blueprint for Objects Created with `new`

- **Nature:** The `prototype` property is found only on constructor functions (functions intended to be used with the new keyword).
- **Role:** It serves as a blueprint for objects created using the new keyword. The `prototype` property of a constructor function becomes the `[[Prototype]]` of the newly created object.
- **Usage:** You define properties and methods on a constructor function's `prototype` property, and those properties and methods become available to all objects created from that constructor.

```
function Animal(name) {
  this.name = name;
}

Animal.prototype.eat = function() {
  console.log(this.name + " is eating.");
};

const dog = new Animal("Buddy");
dog.eat(); // Output: "Buddy is eating."
```

Key Differences

Feature	`__proto__` or `Object.getPrototypeOf()`	`prototype`
Location	Property on objects	Property on constructor functions
Purpose	Access/modify an object's prototype	Defines the prototype for objects created with new
Modification	Can be modified (but discouraged)	Can be modified to affect all instances

Summary

In essence:

- `__proto__` (or `Object.getPrototypeOf()`) is the link between an object and its prototype, allowing for property and method lookup.
- `prototype` is the blueprint used to create objects with new, defining their shared characteristics.

By understanding this distinction, you'll be able to navigate JavaScript's prototypal inheritance system with greater clarity and confidence.

The Power and Flexibility of Prototypal Inheritance

Prototypal inheritance brings a distinct set of advantages and flexibility to JavaScript's object-oriented programming style, setting it apart from traditional class-based inheritance.

Dynamic Nature: Objects Evolve on the Fly

One of the most powerful features of prototypal inheritance is its dynamic nature. Unlike class-based inheritance, where an object's structure is fixed at creation time, JavaScript prototypes can be modified at runtime. This means you can add, remove, or change properties and methods of a prototype, and these changes will instantly be reflected in all objects that inherit from that prototype.

```
function Animal(name) {
  this.name = name;
}

const dog = new Animal("Max");

Animal.prototype.makeSound = function() { // Adding a new method to the
prototype
  console.log("Generic animal sound!");
};

dog.makeSound(); // Output: "Generic animal sound!"
```

This dynamism allows for incredible flexibility and adaptability in your code. You can create objects that evolve over time, responding to changing requirements or user interactions.

Object Composition: Mix and Match Traits

Prototypal inheritance enables a powerful pattern called object composition. Instead of creating deep inheritance hierarchies, you can compose objects by combining features from different prototypes. This allows for greater flexibility and reusability of code.

```
const barker = {
  bark() {
    console.log("Woof!");
  }
};

const swimmer = {
  swim() {
    console.log("Swimming...");
  }
};

const dog = Object.create(animal);
Object.assign(dog, barker, swimmer); // Combining traits from different
prototypes

dog.eat();     // Output: "Max is eating." (Inherited from Animal)
dog.bark();    // Output: "Woof!" (From barker)
dog.swim();  // Output: "Swimming..." (From swimmer)
```

Avoiding Class-Based Inheritance Pitfalls

JavaScript's prototypal inheritance model sidesteps some of the potential pitfalls of class-based inheritance:

- **Fragile Base Class Problem:** Changes to a base class can have unintended consequences on derived classes. In prototypal inheritance, you can modify prototypes without breaking existing objects.
- **Rigid Hierarchy:** Class-based inheritance can lead to deep and rigid hierarchies that are difficult to change. Prototypal inheritance encourages a more flexible and modular approach.

In Summary, prototypes and prototypal inheritance are at the heart of JavaScript's object model. They provide a powerful and flexible mechanism for code reuse, dynamic object behavior, and object composition. By understanding these concepts, you can harness the full power of JavaScript's unique object-oriented capabilities and write cleaner, more maintainable, and more expressive code.

Chapter Summary

In this chapter, we delved into the inner workings of JavaScript's object model, focusing on the powerful concepts of prototypes and inheritance. We explored how every object in JavaScript has a prototype, which serves as a blueprint for its properties and methods. This prototype chain allows objects to inherit characteristics from their ancestors, promoting code reuse and dynamic behavior.

We also clarified the distinction between the `__proto__` property (or `Object.getPrototypeOf()`) and the `prototype` property, understanding their respective roles in the inheritance mechanism.

Furthermore, we explored the advantages of prototypal inheritance, including its dynamic nature, which allows objects to evolve at runtime, and its flexibility in enabling object composition. We also highlighted how prototypal inheritance differs from class-based inheritance and avoids some of its potential pitfalls.

By understanding the concepts covered in this chapter, you have gained a deeper understanding of JavaScript's object-oriented capabilities. This knowledge will be invaluable as you continue your journey to master JavaScript and build more sophisticated applications.

Functions as First-Class Citizens: Higher-Order Functions and Callbacks

Outline

- Functions as Values
- Higher-Order Functions: Functions that Operate on Functions
- Callbacks: Functions as Arguments
- Practical Applications of Higher-Order Functions and Callbacks
- Chapter Summary

Functions as Values

In JavaScript, functions are not merely blocks of code to be executed; they are *first-class citizens*. This means you can treat functions just like any other value (such as numbers, strings, or objects) within your code. You can:

- **Assign them to variables:**

  ```
  const greet = function(name) {
    console.log(`Hello, ${name}!`);
  };
  ```

  Here, `greet` is a variable that holds a function.

- **Pass them as arguments to other functions:**

  ```
  function saySomething(messageFunction) {
    messageFunction("JavaScript is awesome!");
  }

  saySomething(greet); // Output: "Hello, JavaScript is awesome!"
  ```

  The `saySomething` function accepts another function (`messageFunction`) as an argument and calls it.

- **Return them from functions:**

  ```
  function createMultiplier(factor) {
    return function(number) {
      return number * factor;
    };
  }

  const double = createMultiplier(2);
  const triple = createMultiplier(3);

  console.log(double(5)); // Output: 10
  console.log(triple(5)); // Output: 15
  ```

  The `createMultiplier` function returns a new function that multiplies a given number by the specified factor.

- **Store them in data structures (e.g., arrays or objects):**

```
const operations = [
  function(a, b) { return a + b; },
  function(a, b) { return a - b; },
  function(a, b) { return a * b; },
];

console.log(operations[0](2, 3)); // Output: 5
```

Why First-Class Functions Matter

This ability to treat functions as values opens up a world of possibilities:

- **Higher-Order Functions:** You can create functions that accept other functions as arguments or return functions as results. This leads to more expressive and reusable code.
- **Callbacks:** You can pass functions as callbacks to be executed later, enabling asynchronous programming and event-driven behavior.
- **Functional Programming:** First-class functions are the foundation of functional programming paradigms, where you compose complex behaviors from simpler functions.

By understanding the concept of functions as values, you unlock a deeper level of JavaScript's capabilities, enabling you to write more elegant, modular, and powerful code.

Higher-Order Functions: Functions that Operate on Functions

Higher-order functions elevate JavaScript's capabilities by treating functions as data. These specialized functions either accept other functions as arguments (callbacks) or return new functions as their result. This seemingly simple concept unlocks a wealth of benefits, promoting abstraction, code reusability, and a more declarative programming style.

Abstraction: Simplifying Complex Operations

Higher-order functions allow you to abstract away the details of common operations on data structures. Instead of writing repetitive loops to perform tasks like filtering, mapping, or reducing an array, you can use concise higher-order functions that express your intent clearly.

Reusability: Write Once, Use Many Times

By parameterizing the behavior of your code with functions, higher-order functions encourage reusability. You can write a single function that works with different callback functions to perform various tasks on the same data.

Modularity: Breaking Down Complex Logic

Higher-order functions promote modularity by breaking down complex logic into smaller, reusable functions. This makes your code easier to understand, test, and maintain.

Built-in Higher-Order Functions in JavaScript

JavaScript offers several powerful built-in higher-order functions for working with arrays and other data structures:

- **`map(callback)`:** Creates a new array by applying the `callback` function to each element of the original array.

- **`filter(callback)`:** Creates a new array containing only the elements for which the `callback` function returns `true`.
- **`reduce(callback, initialValue)`:** Reduces an array to a single value by applying the `callback` function cumulatively to each element, starting with the `initialValue`.
- **`forEach(callback)`:** Executes the `callback` function for each element of the array.
- **`sort(callback)`:** Sorts an array in place based on the comparison function provided as the `callback`.

Examples in Action

```
const numbers = [1, 2, 3, 4, 5];

const doubled = numbers.map(x => x * 2);     // [2, 4, 6, 8, 10]
const evenNumbers = numbers.filter(x => x % 2 === 0); // [2, 4]

const sum = numbers.reduce((acc, current) => acc + current, 0); // 15

numbers.forEach(x => console.log(x)); // Output: 1 2 3 4 5

numbers.sort((a, b) => a - b);          // Sorts in ascending order
```

Declarative vs. Imperative Style

Higher-order functions encourage a more declarative programming style, where you focus on expressing *what* you want to do rather than *how* to do it. This contrasts with an imperative style, where you explicitly specify the steps of an algorithm using loops and conditionals.

```
// Imperative style
let doubled = [];
for (let i = 0; i < numbers.length; i++) {
  doubled.push(numbers[i] * 2);
}

// Declarative style (using map)
const doubled = numbers.map(x => x * 2);
```

The declarative style is often more concise, readable, and less error-prone.

By understanding and utilizing higher-order functions, you can write cleaner, more maintainable, and more functional JavaScript code. These functions empower you to express your intentions more clearly, abstract away complex operations, and create reusable components for building robust applications.

Callbacks: Functions as Arguments

In JavaScript, a callback is a function that you pass as an argument to another function, with the expectation that the other function will call it back (execute it) at some point in the future. Callbacks are a fundamental mechanism for handling asynchronous operations and events in JavaScript.

Why Callbacks?

JavaScript is single-threaded, meaning it can only do one thing at a time. However, many operations, like fetching data from a server or waiting for a timer to expire, take time to complete. If JavaScript waited for these operations to finish before moving on, your application would freeze and become unresponsive.

Callbacks provide a solution to this problem. By passing a callback function, you tell JavaScript, "When you're done with this task, please execute this function." This allows your code to continue running while the asynchronous operation completes in the background.

Callbacks in Action

Let's explore some common scenarios where callbacks are used:

1. Event Handling:

```
document.getElementById("myButton").addEventListener("click", function() {
  console.log("Button clicked!");
});
```

In this example, the `addEventListener` method registers a callback function that will be executed when the button with the ID "myButton" is clicked.

2. Asynchronous Operations:

```
setTimeout(function() {
  console.log("This message appears after 2 seconds.");
}, 2000);
```

Here, `setTimeout` takes a callback function as its first argument. This function will be executed after the specified delay (2000 milliseconds or 2 seconds).

3. Custom Libraries and Frameworks:

```
function fetchData(url, callback) {
  // ... (code to fetch data from the url) ...
  callback(data);
}

fetchData("/api/users", function(data) {
  // ... (code to process the fetched data) ...
});
```

Many libraries and frameworks provide functions that accept callbacks to customize their behavior. In this example, the `fetchData` function takes a callback that is executed when the data fetching is complete.

Advantages of Callbacks

- **Non-Blocking Code:** Callbacks enable your code to continue executing while asynchronous operations are in progress, preventing your application from becoming unresponsive.
- **Event-Driven Programming:** Callbacks are a key mechanism for responding to events like button clicks, mouse movements, or network responses.
- **Customization:** Libraries and frameworks often use callbacks to allow developers to customize their behavior according to specific needs.

Callback Hell: A Potential Challenge

In complex scenarios, callbacks can lead to a phenomenon known as "callback hell," where you end up with deeply nested callback functions, making code difficult to read and maintain. However, modern JavaScript provides alternatives like Promises and async/await to address this issue.

Key Takeaway

Callbacks are a fundamental concept in JavaScript. They enable asynchronous programming, event handling, and customization, making your code more responsive and adaptable to real-world scenarios. By understanding how callbacks work, you can leverage the full power of JavaScript's event-driven and non-blocking nature.

Practical Applications of Higher-Order Functions and Callbacks

Let's dive into practical scenarios where higher-order functions and callbacks shine, showcasing their ability to simplify complex tasks, enhance code reusability, and improve the structure of your JavaScript projects.

1. Custom Filtering, Sorting, and Mapping on Arrays

Imagine you have an array of products, and you need to:

- Filter products by price range.
- Sort products by name alphabetically.
- Calculate the discounted prices for all products.

Higher-order functions make this a breeze:

```
const products = [
  { name: "Laptop", price: 999.99, discount: 0.1 },
  { name: "Smartphone", price: 599.99, discount: 0.15 },
  { name: "Headphones", price: 129.99, discount: 0.05 }
];

const filtered = products.filter(product => product.price > 500 &&
product.price < 1000);
const sorted = products.sort((a, b) => a.name.localeCompare(b.name));
const discounted = products.map(product => ({
  ...product,
  discountedPrice: product.price * (1 - product.discount)
}));
```

2. Reusable Functions for Different Data Types

Higher-order functions allow you to create versatile functions that work with various data types by accepting callback functions that handle the specific logic.

```
function processData(data, operation) {
  return data.map(operation);
}

const numbers = [1, 2, 3];
const doubledNumbers = processData(numbers, x => x * 2);

const words = ["apple", "banana", "orange"];
const capitalizedWords = processData(words, word => word.toUpperCase());
```

Here, `processData` can handle both numbers and strings, thanks to the `operation` callback.

3. Organized Asynchronous Operations

Callbacks play a crucial role in managing asynchronous operations, such as fetching data from an API.

```
function fetchData(url, callback) {
  fetch(url)
    .then(response => response.json())
    .then(data => callback(null, data))
    .catch(error => callback(error));
}

fetchData("/api/posts", function(error, posts) {
  if (error) {
    console.error("Error fetching data:", error);
  } else {
    // Process the fetched posts
  }
});
```

The callback pattern provides a structured way to handle success and error scenarios when dealing with asynchronous tasks.

4. Flexible APIs and Libraries

Many JavaScript libraries and frameworks heavily rely on callbacks and higher-order functions to enable customization and extensibility.

```
const express = require('express');
const app = express();

app.get('/', function(req, res) {
  res.send('Hello World!');
});
```

In Express.js, a popular web framework, route handlers are callback functions executed when specific URLs are requested.

By incorporating higher-order functions and callbacks into your code, you'll benefit from:

- **Improved Readability:** Code becomes more concise and focused on the desired outcome.
- **Enhanced Maintainability:** Reusable functions and modular structure make changes easier.
- **Increased Flexibility:** Your code can adapt to different data types and scenarios.

These practical applications demonstrate the significant advantages of leveraging higher-order functions and callbacks in real-world JavaScript development.

Chapter Summary

In this chapter, we delved into the power of functions as first-class citizens in JavaScript. We explored how functions can be treated as values, assigned to variables, passed as arguments, and returned from other functions. This fundamental concept opens the door to higher-order functions, which are functions that operate on other functions.

We examined how higher-order functions like `map`, `filter`, and `reduce` can transform arrays and other data structures in a concise and declarative manner. We also discussed callbacks, which are functions passed as arguments to be executed later, typically used for handling events and asynchronous operations.

Through practical examples, we demonstrated how higher-order functions and callbacks can be applied to create custom data processing operations, build reusable functions, manage asynchronous tasks, and design flexible APIs. These techniques enhance code readability, maintainability, and flexibility, making them indispensable tools in modern JavaScript development.

By mastering these concepts, you have acquired valuable skills for writing more functional, expressive, and efficient JavaScript code. This knowledge will serve you well as you tackle more advanced challenges in your JavaScript journey.

Section III:
Deep Dive into Scope and Closures

Scope Demystified: Global, Local, and Block Scope

Outline

- What is Scope?
- Global Scope: The Universal Container
- Local Scope: Function-Level Privacy
- Block Scope: Fine-Grained Control with `let` and `const`
- Scope Chain: The Hierarchical Lookup
- Lexical Scope: Where Variables Live
- Common Scope-Related Mistakes
- Chapter Summary

What is Scope?

Imagine your JavaScript code as a house with several rooms. Each room represents a different scope, a distinct area where variables can exist and be accessed. Just as you wouldn't expect to find your bedroom belongings in the kitchen, variables declared in one scope aren't automatically visible in another.

Scope as Containers

Think of scopes as nested containers:

```
Global Scope (Biggest Container)
 └── Function Scope (Smaller Container)
      └── Block Scope (Smallest Container)
```

- **Global Scope:** This is the outermost container, like the entire house. Variables declared here are accessible from any room.
- **Local Scope (Function Scope):** Each function creates its own room. Variables declared inside a function are only visible within that room.
- **Block Scope:** Introduced in ES6 (ECMAScript 2015), blocks of code (like those in `if` statements, loops, or standalone `{}`) also create their own tiny rooms within a function.

Scope's Role in Your Code

Scope acts as a gatekeeper, controlling which variables are accessible in different parts of your program. This is crucial for several reasons:

- **Variable Name Management:** You can use the same variable name in different scopes without conflicts. Each scope has its own set of variables, like having a "cupboard" in each room of the house.
- **Avoiding Unintended Side Effects:** Scope prevents variables from being accidentally modified from other parts of your code. This ensures that your variables behave as you expect.

- **Code Organization:** Scope helps you organize your code into logical units (functions and blocks). Each unit has its own set of variables, making your code easier to understand and maintain.
- **Predictability:** By knowing the scope of a variable, you can predict where it can be used and how it will interact with other parts of your code.

A Simple Example

```
let globalVar = "I'm global";

function myFunction() {
  let localVar = "I'm local";
  console.log(globalVar); // Accessible (from outer scope)
  console.log(localVar);  // Accessible (in the same scope)
}

myFunction();
console.log(localVar); // Error! localVar is not accessible outside the
function
```

In this example, `globalVar` is accessible both inside and outside the function because it's in the global scope. However, `localVar` is only accessible within `myFunction()` because it's in a local scope.

The Importance of Understanding Scope

Mastering scope is fundamental for writing clean, maintainable, and bug-free JavaScript code. By understanding the rules of scope, you can write code that is more predictable, reusable, and easier to reason about. In the following sections, we'll delve deeper into the different types of scope and their nuances in JavaScript.

Global Scope: The Universal Container

Think of the global scope as the vast expanse of the JavaScript universe. It's the outermost layer, encompassing everything else within your code. Any variable or function declared in this global space becomes a cosmic citizen, accessible from any corner of your program.

Declaring Global Variables

You create global variables by declaring them outside of any function or block (a set of statements enclosed in curly braces `{}`). Here's how:

```
var globalName = "Earth";
let globalAge = 4.543; // Billions of years old!
const globalGravity = 9.81; // m/s²
```

These variables are now part of the global scope and can be used freely throughout your code:

```
function calculateWeight(mass) {
  return mass * globalGravity;
}

console.log(globalName);            // Output: "Earth"
console.log(calculateWeight(70));    // Output: 686.7 (uses globalGravity)
```

The Global Object

In web browsers, the global scope is represented by the `window` object. In Node.js environments, it's called `global`. So, our global variables `globalName`, `globalAge`, and `globalGravity` would become properties of the `window` (or `global`) object.

The Dark Side of Global Variables: Proceed with Caution!

While global variables offer convenience, they come with some significant drawbacks if used excessively:

1. **Namespace Pollution:** As your codebase grows, the global scope can become cluttered with variables. This increases the risk of naming conflicts and makes it harder to reason about your code.
2. **Unintended Side Effects:** Because global variables can be modified from anywhere, it's easy to accidentally introduce bugs when one part of your code unknowingly changes a global variable that another part relies on.
3. **Difficulty in Testing:** Global variables can make it harder to write isolated unit tests for your code.

Best Practices: Use Global Variables Sparingly

- **Favor Local Variables:** Whenever possible, declare variables within functions or blocks to limit their scope.
- **Modules:** Use modules (covered later in the book) to encapsulate code and manage global variables more effectively.
- **Constants:** If you need a global value that shouldn't change, use `const` to make it immutable.
- **Naming Conventions:** Use clear and descriptive names for global variables to avoid conflicts (e.g., prefix them with "g_" or "GLOBAL_").

By understanding the global scope and its potential pitfalls, you can make informed decisions about when to use global variables and how to manage them effectively to maintain a clean and maintainable codebase.

Local Scope: Function-Level Privacy

Local scope is like a private room within your JavaScript house. Every time you define a function, you're essentially building a new room with its own set of rules. Variables declared inside this room using `var`, `let`, or `const` are exclusive to that room—they are local variables and cannot be accessed or modified from outside.

Encapsulation: Keeping Things Tidy

This concept of local scope is crucial for encapsulation. Encapsulation means bundling data and the functions that operate on that data together. Local variables help achieve this by keeping data private and preventing unintended access from other parts of your code. This reduces the risk of errors caused by accidental modification and makes your code more modular and maintainable.

Example: A Function's Inner Sanctum

```
function calculateArea(width, height) {
  let area = width * height; // Local variable
  console.log(`The area is: ${area}`);
}

calculateArea(5, 10); // Output: "The area is: 50"
console.log(area);    // Error! 'area' is not defined (outside the function)
```

In this example:

1. The `calculateArea` function defines a local variable `area` within its scope.
2. The function calculates the area and logs it to the console.
3. Outside the function, trying to access `area` results in an error because it's a local variable and doesn't exist in the global scope.

Accessing and Modifying Local Variables

You can access and modify local variables freely within the function's body:

```
function countToTen() {
  let count = 1;
  while (count <= 10) {
    console.log(count);
    count++;
  }
}

countToTen();
```

In this loop, the `count` variable is local to the `countToTen` function and is only accessible within the loop.

Why Local Scope Matters

- **Data Protection:** Local variables are shielded from external interference, preventing bugs caused by accidental modification.
- **Code Reusability:** Functions with local variables can be used in different contexts without worrying about variable name clashes.
- **Memory Management:** Local variables are automatically destroyed when the function finishes executing, freeing up memory resources.

By understanding and using local scope effectively, you'll be able to write more organized, robust, and maintainable JavaScript code.

Block Scope: Fine-Grained Control with `let` and `const`

In modern JavaScript (ES6 and later), block scope offers even finer control over variable accessibility. Unlike `var`, which is function-scoped or globally scoped, variables declared with `let` and `const` have block scope. This means their visibility is limited to the specific block of code (delimited by curly braces `{}`) in which they are defined.

Blocks: More Than Just Functions

Blocks of code are everywhere in JavaScript. They are not limited to functions. You encounter them in:

- **Conditional Statements (`if`, `else if`, `else`)**
- **Loops (`for`, `while`, `do...while`)**
- **Standalone Blocks:** You can create blocks explicitly using curly braces.

```
if (true) {
  let blockVar = "I'm block-scoped";
  console.log(blockVar); // Accessible within this block
}
console.log(blockVar);    // Error! blockVar is not accessible here
```

In this example, `blockVar` is declared inside an `if` statement's block and is only accessible within that block.

Benefits of Block Scope

- **Enhanced Encapsulation:** Block scope provides a more precise way to control variable visibility, further promoting encapsulation and preventing unintended side effects.
- **Avoiding Variable Hoisting Issues:** Variables declared with `let` and `const` are not hoisted in the same way as `var` variables. This means you cannot access them before their declaration within the block, making your code more predictable.
- **Minimizing Variable Lifetime:** Variables with block scope exist only within their respective block, reducing the chances of memory leaks and improving code clarity.

Example: Block Scope in a Loop

```
for (let i = 0; i < 5; i++) {
  let message = `Iteration ${i}`;
  console.log(message); // Accessible within this loop iteration
}

console.log(message);    // Error! message is not accessible outside the loop
console.log(i);          // Error! i is also not accessible outside the loop
```

Here, both `i` and `message` are block-scoped to each iteration of the loop. They are not accessible outside the loop.

Embrace Block Scope

By using `let` and `const` and understanding block scope, you can write cleaner, more maintainable, and less error-prone JavaScript code. Embrace block scope as a powerful tool for managing your variables and ensuring that your code behaves as expected.

Scope Chain: The Hierarchical Lookup

Imagine you're trying to find a book in a library. You start by searching the current shelf. If it's not there, you move to the next shelf, then the next aisle, and eventually, the entire library. JavaScript's scope chain works similarly when it searches for a variable.

Nested Scopes: A Hierarchy of Access

JavaScript scopes can be nested within each other, forming a hierarchical structure called the scope chain. Each scope has access to variables declared within itself and in any of its outer (parent) scopes.

```
Global Scope
 └── Function A
     └── Function B
         └── Block C
```

In this example, Block C can access variables from Function B, Function A, and the Global Scope. Function B can access variables from Function A and the Global Scope. Function A can only access variables from the Global Scope.

The Lookup Process: Climbing the Ladder

When you try to access a variable in JavaScript, the engine follows a specific search pattern:

1. **Current Scope:** It first looks for the variable in the current scope (e.g., the block or function where the variable is used).
2. **Parent Scope:** If not found, it moves up to the parent scope (the enclosing function or block).
3. **Grandparent Scope (and so on):** It continues up the chain of scopes, checking each ancestor until it reaches the global scope.
4. **Global Scope:** Finally, it checks the global scope. If the variable is still not found, JavaScript throws a `ReferenceError`.

Visualizing the Scope Chain

```
// Code Example
let outerVar = "I'm outside!";

function outerFunction() {
  let innerVar = "I'm inside!";

  function innerFunction() {
    console.log(outerVar); // Output: "I'm outside!"
    console.log(innerVar); // Output: "I'm inside!"
  }

  innerFunction();
}

outerFunction();

// Scope Chain Diagram
Global Scope (outerVar)
  └── outerFunction (innerVar)
        └── innerFunction
```

In this illustration, `innerFunction` can access both `outerVar` (from the global scope) and `innerVar` (from its parent function's scope).

Why Scope Chain Matters

- **Variable Resolution:** The scope chain determines how JavaScript resolves variable references, ensuring that the correct value is used.
- **Encapsulation:** It enforces encapsulation by preventing access to variables outside their intended scope.
- **Predictability:** Understanding the scope chain helps you predict how your code will behave and avoid unexpected errors.

By grasping the concept of scope chain, you gain a deeper understanding of how JavaScript manages variables and their accessibility. This knowledge is fundamental for writing well-structured, maintainable, and error-free code.

Lexical Scope: Where Variables Live

Lexical scope, also known as static scope, is a fundamental concept in JavaScript that determines the visibility and accessibility of variables within your code. It's like a variable's home address, fixed at the time you write your code and not subject to change during execution.

Scope by Position: The Lexical Environment

In JavaScript, a variable's scope is determined by where it's declared in the source code. Each block of code (delimited by curly braces {}) creates a new lexical environment. This environment keeps track of the variables declared within it.

When JavaScript encounters a variable reference, it first looks for it in the current lexical environment. If it's not found there, it moves outward to the parent lexical environment, then to its parent, and so on, all the way up to the global scope. This chain of lexical environments is what we call the scope chain.

The Time of Writing, Not Execution

Lexical scope is statically determined, meaning it's established when you write your code, not when you run it. This makes your code more predictable because you can easily trace where a variable is defined and where it can be accessed based on its position in the code structure.

Nested Functions and Lexical Scope

Nested functions are a key feature in JavaScript. They demonstrate the power of lexical scope. A nested function has access to the variables declared in its own scope, as well as the variables declared in its outer (parent) scopes.

```
function outerFunction() {
  let outerVar = 10;

  function innerFunction() {
    let innerVar = 20;
    console.log(outerVar); // Accessing outerVar from the outer scope
    console.log(innerVar); // Accessing innerVar from the inner scope
  }

  innerFunction();
}

outerFunction();
```

In this example:

- The `innerFunction` can access both `outerVar` (from its parent function's scope) and `innerVar` (from its own scope).
- The `outerFunction` can access `outerVar`, but not `innerVar` (because it's declared in a nested scope).
- Outside of both functions, neither variable is accessible.

Why Lexical Scope Matters

Lexical scope provides several benefits:

- **Readability:** You can easily determine the scope of a variable by looking at its declaration in the code.
- **Maintainability:** Code is more organized and easier to reason about when variables are scoped appropriately.
- **Encapsulation:** Lexical scope helps to encapsulate data, preventing accidental modification from other parts of the code.
- **Closure Formation:** Lexical scope plays a crucial role in the creation of closures, which we'll explore in the next chapter.

By understanding lexical scope, you'll gain a deeper understanding of how JavaScript manages variables and how to write code that is more predictable, modular, and easier to maintain.

Common Scope-Related Mistakes

Even with a solid understanding of scope, it's easy to fall into traps that lead to unexpected behavior or errors. Let's explore some common mistakes and how to avoid them:

1. Accidental Global Variables: The Undeclared Menace

Forgetting to declare a variable using `var`, `let`, or `const` doesn't mean your code won't run. Instead, JavaScript implicitly creates a global variable for you. This can lead to namespace pollution and unexpected interactions between different parts of your code.

```
function myFunction() {
  undeclaredVar = 10; // Oops! Forgot 'let' or 'const'
}
myFunction();
console.log(undeclaredVar); // Output: 10 (global variable)
```

How to Avoid: Always declare your variables explicitly using `let` or `const` (and avoid `var` in modern JavaScript). This ensures they have the correct scope and prevents accidental globals.

2. Shadowing: The Variable Imposter

When you declare a variable with the same name in a nested scope as a variable in an outer scope, you're essentially creating a "shadow" variable. The outer variable becomes hidden within the inner scope, leading to potential confusion.

```
let message = "Hello from the outside!";

function sayHello() {
  let message = "Hello from inside!";
  console.log(message); // Output: "Hello from inside!"
}

sayHello();
console.log(message); // Output: "Hello from the outside!"
```

How to Avoid: Be mindful of variable names, especially when dealing with nested functions or blocks. Consider using different names to avoid shadowing or explicitly referencing the outer variable using a different identifier.

3. Modified Closures: The Changing Landscape

Closures, a powerful feature we'll explore in depth later, can also lead to unexpected behavior when combined with variable modification. A closure captures variables from its surrounding scope, but it captures them by reference, not by value.

```
let counter = 0;

function createCounter() {
  return function() {
    counter++;
    console.log(counter);
```

```
    };
}

const increment = createCounter();
increment(); // Output: 1
increment(); // Output: 2
```

How to Avoid: Be aware that closures capture variables by reference. If you need to preserve a value, consider creating a copy of the variable inside the closure or using techniques like immediately invoked function expressions (IIFEs) to create new scopes.

Best Practices: Keep Your Scope Clean

- **Use Strict Mode:** Enable strict mode using `"use strict";` at the beginning of your scripts. Strict mode helps catch accidental global variables and other common mistakes.
- **Declare Variables Explicitly:** Always use `let` or `const` (and avoid `var`) to declare variables. This ensures they have the correct scope and prevents accidental globals.
- **Mind Your Naming:** Be mindful of variable names, especially in nested scopes, to avoid shadowing.
- **Closures with Care:** Understand how closures capture variables and be cautious when modifying variables from outer scopes within a closure.

By following these best practices and understanding the common pitfalls, you can navigate the world of JavaScript scope with confidence, writing cleaner, more reliable, and more predictable code.

Chapter Summary

In this chapter, we've embarked on a journey to demystify the concept of scope in JavaScript. We explored how scope acts as a set of rules that govern the accessibility of variables within your code, acting like rooms in a house with varying levels of privacy.

We started by defining global scope as the all-encompassing space where variables are accessible from anywhere in your code, while highlighting the potential drawbacks of overuse. We then delved into local (function) scope, a more private space where variables are confined to their respective functions. Building on that, we introduced block scope, a more fine-grained control mechanism enabled by `let` and `const`, further enhancing encapsulation.

We also explored the concept of scope chain, the hierarchical structure that JavaScript uses to search for variables. Understanding how the scope chain works is crucial for predicting how your code will behave. Additionally, we discussed lexical scope, emphasizing that scope is determined at the time you write your code, not when it runs.

Finally, we addressed common scope-related mistakes that even seasoned developers can encounter, such as accidental global variables, shadowing, and unexpected closure behavior. By following best practices like using strict mode, declaring variables explicitly, and being mindful of variable names, you can avoid these pitfalls and write cleaner, more reliable code.

Mastering scope is a fundamental step toward becoming a proficient JavaScript developer. By understanding the rules that govern variable visibility and accessibility, you'll be well-equipped to write code that is organized, maintainable, and free from unexpected surprises.

The Power of Closures: Functions That "Remember" Their Surroundings

Outline

- What is a Closure?
- How Closures Work: Lexical Scoping and Inner Functions
- The Closure's Backpack: Remembering Variables
- Practical Applications of Closures
- Chapter Summary

What is a Closure?

In the intricate world of JavaScript, closures are a fascinating phenomenon. At its core, a closure is simply a function's ability to "remember" the variables and functions that existed in the environment where it was created, even after the outer function has completed its execution.

Think of a closure as a function with a backpack. When it's created, it packs all the variables and functions from its surrounding scope into its backpack. Even if the outer function goes away (finishes executing), the inner function still has access to everything it packed away.

Not Just a Snapshot

It's important to note that this "memory" is not a snapshot of the values at the time the closure is formed. It's a live connection. If the values of those outer variables change, the closure will see those changes when it accesses them later.

A Simple Example

```
function outerFunction(name) {
  let message = "Hello, " + name + "!";

  function innerFunction() {
    console.log(message); // Accessing 'message' from outerFunction
  }

  return innerFunction; // Returning the inner function
}

let greetAlice = outerFunction("Alice");
greetAlice(); // Output: "Hello, Alice!"
```

Here's what's happening:

1. `outerFunction` is called with the argument "Alice." It creates a local variable `message`.
2. The `innerFunction` is defined within `outerFunction`. It forms a closure, capturing the `message` variable in its backpack.
3. `outerFunction` returns `innerFunction`.
4. The returned `innerFunction` is assigned to `greetAlice`.
5. When `greetAlice()` is called, it remembers the `message` variable from its creation environment and logs "Hello, Alice!"

The Magic of Closures

Closures might seem like magic, but they're a fundamental mechanism that underpins many powerful features of JavaScript:

- **Data Encapsulation:** Closures can be used to create private variables, hiding data from the outside world.
- **State Preservation:** Callbacks in event handlers or asynchronous operations can use closures to maintain their state.
- **Partial Application and Currying:** These functional programming techniques rely on closures to create more specialized functions.

Understanding closures is essential for writing more advanced JavaScript code. They enable you to create functions that are more flexible, modular, and expressive.

How Closures Work: Lexical Scoping and Inner Functions

Closures come to life through the interplay of nested functions and lexical scoping. Let's break down how this works.

Nested Functions: Functions within Functions

A nested function is simply a function defined inside another function. It's like a smaller room within a larger house. The inner function has access to the variables and functions declared within its own scope, but it also has a special ability: it can reach out and access the variables of its outer (parent) function.

Lexical Scoping: The Rules of the Game

This ability to access outer variables is due to a concept called lexical scoping. Lexical scope means that the scope of a variable is determined by its location in the source code, specifically where it's declared. When a nested function is created, it essentially takes a snapshot of the surrounding lexical environment at the time of its creation. This snapshot includes all the variables and functions that are accessible within its outer function.

Code Example: Closure in Practice

```
function outerFunction(name) {
  let greeting = "Hello";

  function innerFunction() {
    console.log(greeting + ", " + name + "!");
  }

  return innerFunction;
}

const greetBob = outerFunction("Bob"); // Creates a closure
greetBob(); // Output: "Hello, Bob!"
```

1. **Outer Function:** `outerFunction` is called with the argument "Bob." It defines a variable `greeting` and a nested function `innerFunction`.
2. **Inner Function:** `innerFunction` is defined within the scope of `outerFunction`. Due to lexical scoping, it has access to the `greeting` variable from its outer scope.

3. **Closure Creation:** `outerFunction` returns `innerFunction`. At this point, a closure is created. `innerFunction` is packaged together with its lexical environment (including the `greeting` variable).
4. **Calling the Closure:** The returned function is assigned to `greetBob`. When you call `greetBob()`, it remembers the value of `greeting` from its closure and uses it to log the message.

Key Points:

- **Lexical Environment:** A closure "remembers" its lexical environment, which is the collection of variables and functions that were in scope when the closure was created.
- **Lifetime of Variables:** Even after the outer function finishes executing, the variables within the closure remain in memory as long as the closure exists.
- **Data Encapsulation:** Closures provide a way to encapsulate data. The variables within a closure are only accessible to the inner function, protecting them from being modified by external code.

By understanding how closures work and how they leverage lexical scoping, you can harness their power to create more expressive, modular, and reusable JavaScript code.

The Closure's Backpack: Remembering Variables

Imagine a function as a traveler embarking on a journey. When a function is defined within another function (nested), it packs a special backpack—the closure—before setting off. Inside this backpack, it carefully stores all the variables and functions from its surrounding environment.

Packing the Essentials

As the inner function travels through your code, it carries its backpack with it. Even if the outer function (the original starting point) disappears, the inner function still has access to the contents of its backpack. It can reach in and use those variables or functions whenever it needs them, just like a traveler relying on the supplies they packed for the journey.

Live References, Not Just Copies

The crucial point here is that the closure doesn't just make copies of the variables; it holds *live references* to them. This means that if the original variables change, the closure will see those updated values.

Code Example: The Counting Backpack

```
function createCounter() {
  let count = 0; // The variable in the backpack

  return function() {
    count++;
    console.log(count);
  };
}

const counter1 = createCounter();
const counter2 = createCounter();

counter1(); // Output: 1
counter1(); // Output: 2

counter2(); // Output: 1 (Each closure has its own independent 'count')
```

In this example:

1. `createCounter` creates a new closure each time it's called. Each closure gets its own independent "backpack" containing the `count` variable.
2. The inner function increments `count` and logs it to the console.
3. Even though `createCounter` has finished executing, the `count` variables continue to exist within each closure's backpack.
4. Each closure maintains its own separate count, illustrating how closures create independent environments.

Changing the Contents of the Backpack

The variables within a closure can be modified from within the inner function. This demonstrates the live nature of the references.

```
function createMultiplier(factor) {
  let result = 1;
  return function(number) {
    result *= number; // Modifying the variable in the backpack
    console.log(result * factor);
  };
}

const multiplyByFive = createMultiplier(5);
multiplyByFive(2); // Output: 10
multiplyByFive(3); // Output: 150 (result is retained)
```

In this case, the inner function multiplies the `result` variable by the input number and the constant factor, showcasing the persistent memory of the closure.

Key Takeaways

- Closures create a "backpack" of variables from their lexical environment.
- These variables are live references, not copies.
- You can modify the variables within the backpack from the inner function.
- Each closure has its own independent backpack, maintaining separate state.

By understanding how closures work as backpacks, you can leverage them effectively for data encapsulation, state preservation, and creating more complex function behaviors in JavaScript.

Practical Applications of Closures

Closures are not merely a theoretical concept; they are a powerful tool with practical applications that can elevate your JavaScript code to the next level. Let's explore some real-world scenarios where closures shine:

1. Data Encapsulation and Privacy

In object-oriented programming, encapsulation is the practice of bundling data (properties) and the operations that work on that data (methods) together within an object. This helps protect data from accidental modification and provides a clear interface for interacting with it.

Closures are a key enabler of encapsulation in JavaScript. They allow you to create private variables and methods within a function, effectively shielding them from the outside world. The inner functions become the only way to access and manipulate these private values.

Example: A Private Counter

```
function createCounter() {
  let count = 0; // Private variable

  return {
    increment: function() {
      count++;
    },
    get: function() {
      return count;
    }
  };
}

const counter = createCounter();

counter.increment();
counter.increment();
console.log(counter.get()); // Output: 2
console.log(count);        // Error! 'count' is not defined (it's private)
```

In this example:

1. The `createCounter` function defines a private variable `count`.
2. It returns an object with two methods: `increment` (to increase the count) and `get` (to retrieve the current count).
3. The returned object acts as the public interface to the counter.
4. The `count` variable is inaccessible from outside the closure, ensuring its privacy and preventing accidental changes.

This pattern is often used to create modules, libraries, or objects with private data and methods. It helps to maintain the integrity of data, prevent unintended modifications, and create a more controlled and predictable environment for your code.

2. State Preservation in Event Handlers

In the dynamic world of web applications, event handlers are essential for responding to user interactions like clicks, hovers, and form submissions. Often, these event handlers need to remember the state of variables at the time the event was attached, not just the current state when the handler is executed. This is where closures become indispensable.

The Challenge: Changing Variables

Consider this scenario: you have a set of buttons dynamically generated by JavaScript. Each button should display its unique identifier when clicked. A naive approach might look like this:

```
for (let i = 0; i < 5; i++) {
  let button = document.createElement("button");
  button.textContent = "Button " + i;

  button.addEventListener("click", function() {
    console.log("Button " + i + " clicked!"); // Problem: 'i' will always be 5
  });

  document.body.appendChild(button);
```

```
}
```

However, this code won't work as expected. When a button is clicked, it will always log "Button 5 clicked!" Why? Because the event handler function runs after the loop has completed, and by that time, the value of `i` is 5 for all buttons.

Closures: Preserving the State

The solution lies in using a closure. A closure allows the event handler function to "remember" the value of `i` at the time the event listener was attached.

```
for (let i = 0; i < 5; i++) {
  let button = document.createElement("button");
  button.textContent = "Button " + i;

  button.addEventListener("click", (function(index) { // IIFE to create a
closure
    return function() {
      console.log("Button " + index + " clicked!"); // 'index' is preserved
    };
  })(i)); // Immediately pass 'i' to the IIFE

  document.body.appendChild(button);
}
```

In this improved version:

1. We use an Immediately Invoked Function Expression (IIFE) to create a new scope for each button.
2. The IIFE takes `i` as an argument (now called `index`).
3. It returns a new function (the event handler) that has access to the `index` variable from the IIFE's scope.
4. When the button is clicked, the event handler uses the correct `index` value, thanks to the closure.

Closures as Time Capsules

Think of the closure as a time capsule. It captures the state of variables at a specific point in time, ensuring that those values are preserved even when the surrounding environment changes. This makes closures incredibly valuable in event handling, where you need to maintain the context of the event that triggered the callback.

Beyond Buttons: More Applications

Closures are not just for buttons. They are essential whenever you need a function to remember its surrounding state, such as:

- **Timers (setTimeout, setInterval):** Callbacks in timers can use closures to track time or maintain state between ticks.
- **Asynchronous Operations:** Callbacks for AJAX requests or Promise resolutions can use closures to access data from the original request context.
- **Partial Application and Currying:** Closures enable these functional programming techniques, where functions return specialized versions of themselves with some arguments pre-filled.

By understanding how closures work and how they preserve state, you can write more robust and reliable event handlers and leverage the full power of asynchronous programming in JavaScript.

3. Partial Application and Currying

Closures are not just about privacy and state; they also enable powerful functional programming techniques known as partial application and currying. These techniques allow you to create specialized versions of functions, enhancing code reusability and flexibility.

Partial Application: Fixing Arguments

Partial application involves creating a new function by fixing some of the arguments of an existing function. The returned function takes the remaining arguments and calls the original function with all arguments combined.

```
function greet(greeting, name) {
  console.log(greeting + ", " + name + "!");
}

const sayHelloTo = greet.bind(null, "Hello"); // Partial application with
'Hello' fixed

sayHelloTo("Alice"); // Output: "Hello, Alice!"
sayHelloTo("Bob");   // Output: "Hello, Bob!"
```

Here, `greet.bind(null, "Hello")` creates a new function `sayHelloTo` with the `greeting` argument fixed as "Hello." This new function only takes one argument (the name) and calls the original `greet` function with both arguments.

Currying: Functions Chaining Together

Currying goes a step further than partial application. It transforms a function with multiple arguments into a sequence of nested functions, each taking a single argument. The final function in the chain is executed when all arguments are provided.

```
function curryGreet(greeting) {
  return function(name) {
    console.log(greeting + ", " + name + "!");
  };
}

const sayHello = curryGreet("Hello");
sayHello("Alice"); // Output: "Hello, Alice!"

const sayHi = curryGreet("Hi");
sayHi("Bob");     // Output: "Hi, Bob!"
```

Here, `curryGreet` takes a `greeting` argument and returns a function that takes a `name` argument. By calling `curryGreet("Hello")`, we get a specialized function `sayHello` that always uses "Hello" as the greeting.

The Role of Closures

Both partial application and currying rely on closures. The returned functions from these techniques form closures that capture the values of the arguments passed to the original function. This allows you to create specialized functions without having to repeatedly pass the same arguments.

Advantages of Partial Application and Currying

- **Flexibility:** You can create variations of a function on the fly, tailoring it to specific needs.

- **Reusability:** You can reuse the same function for different tasks by partially applying or currying its arguments.
- **Composition:** You can create complex functions by composing simpler functions together using these techniques.

By understanding partial application and currying, you'll be able to write more concise, expressive, and adaptable code that embraces the full power of functional programming in JavaScript.

4. Module Pattern

The module pattern is a time-tested design pattern in JavaScript that enables you to create modular and encapsulated code. It leverages closures to provide privacy for variables and functions, exposing only a carefully controlled public interface. This pattern is essential for building maintainable and scalable applications.

What is a Module?

In the context of JavaScript, a module is a self-contained unit of code that encapsulates related functionality. It has its own private data and functions, which are hidden from the outside world, and it exposes a public API that other parts of your code can interact with.

The Role of Closures

Closures play a crucial role in the module pattern. They allow you to define private variables and functions within a module, which can only be accessed and modified from within the module itself. The public API, on the other hand, is returned as a function or an object, and it can access and manipulate the private data through closures.

Example: A Shopping Cart Module

Let's see how to create a reusable shopping cart module using the module pattern:

```
const shoppingCartModule = (function() {
  let items = [];

  function addItem(item) {
    items.push(item);
  }

  function removeItem(item) {
    const index = items.indexOf(item);
    if (index > -1) {
      items.splice(index, 1);
    }
  }

  function getTotal() {
    return items.reduce((total, item) => total + item.price, 0);
  }

  return {
    addItem: addItem,
    removeItem: removeItem,
    getTotal: getTotal
  };
})();
```

```
shoppingCartModule.addItem({ name: "Laptop", price: 999.99 });
shoppingCartModule.addItem({ name: "Smartphone", price: 599.99 });
console.log(shoppingCartModule.getTotal()); // Output: 1599.98
```

In this module:

- `items` is a private array that stores the cart items.
- `addItem`, `removeItem`, and `getTotal` are private functions for manipulating the cart.
- The returned object provides the public API, consisting of references to these private functions.

Advantages of the Module Pattern

- **Encapsulation:** Protects private data and functions from external interference.
- **Reusability:** Modules can be used in multiple parts of your application or even in different projects.
- **Organization:** Code is structured into logical units, improving maintainability.
- **Global Namespace Protection:** Prevents accidental pollution of the global namespace.

Modern Alternatives: ES Modules

While the module pattern has been a staple in JavaScript for a long time, ES6 (ECMAScript 2015) introduced a standardized module system. ES modules offer a more concise and structured way to define and consume modules, but they rely on modern JavaScript environments that support them.

By understanding the module pattern, you'll gain a deeper understanding of JavaScript's modularity and how closures can be leveraged to create encapsulated, reusable, and maintainable code. This pattern remains relevant even with the introduction of ES modules, as it can be used in environments that don't yet fully support the new module system.

Chapter Summary

In this chapter, we explored the remarkable power of closures in JavaScript. We learned how closures allow functions to retain access to variables from their surrounding scope, even after the outer functions have completed. This unique ability, made possible by lexical scoping, opens doors to a wide range of practical applications.

We delved into how closures enable data encapsulation and privacy, allowing you to create modules with hidden variables and functions, accessible only through a controlled public interface. We also saw how closures are essential for preserving state in event handlers, ensuring that callback functions have access to the correct values even when variables change over time.

Moreover, we discovered how closures underpin functional programming techniques like partial application and currying, enabling the creation of more specialized and reusable functions. Finally, we examined the classic module pattern, a powerful design pattern that leverages closures to create encapsulated, reusable modules.

By mastering closures, you've added a valuable tool to your JavaScript skillset. You can now write more expressive, modular, and maintainable code, effectively manage state in asynchronous operations, and build more complex applications with confidence.

Closures in Practice: Modules, Private Variables, and Event Handling

Outline

- Modules: Building Blocks with Closures
- Private Variables: Keeping Secrets with Closures
- Event Handling: Closures and Persistent State
- Common Closure Pitfalls: Memory Leaks and `this`
- Chapter Summary

Modules: Building Blocks with Closures

In the world of software development, modularity is key to creating well-structured, maintainable, and scalable applications. JavaScript, traditionally a language without built-in modules, found a clever workaround using closures: the Module Pattern.

What Makes a Module?

A module is a self-contained unit of code that encapsulates specific functionality. Think of it as a black box with a well-defined interface. It hides its inner workings (private members) and exposes only what's necessary for the outside world to interact with (public API).

Closures as Encapsulation Engines

Closures are the secret sauce that makes modules possible in JavaScript. By leveraging closures, you can create private variables and functions within a module, shielding them from external access. Only the public API, which typically consists of functions or objects returned by the module, can interact with these private members.

The Module Pattern: A Classic Solution

The Module Pattern is a widely used approach to create modules in JavaScript. It involves wrapping the module's code in an Immediately Invoked Function Expression (IIFE), creating a closure that encapsulates the private members.

```
const counterModule = (function() {
  let count = 0; // Private variable

  function increment() {
    count++;
  }

  function decrement() {
    count--;
  }

  function getValue() {
    return count;
  }

  return {
    increment: increment,
```

```
    decrement: decrement,
    getValue: getValue
  };
})();
```

In this example:

1. The IIFE (`(function() { ... })()`) creates a new scope, forming a closure.
2. Inside the closure, `count` is a private variable, inaccessible from the outside.
3. `increment`, `decrement`, and `getValue` are private functions that operate on `count`.
4. The IIFE returns an object containing references to the `increment`, `decrement`, and `getValue` functions. This object becomes the module's public API.

Now, you can interact with the counter module through its public API:

```
counterModule.increment();
counterModule.increment();
console.log(counterModule.getValue()); // Output: 2

counterModule.decrement();
console.log(counterModule.getValue()); // Output: 1
```

You cannot access `count` directly:

```
console.log(counterModule.count); // Output: undefined
```

Advantages of the Module Pattern

- **Encapsulation:** Private data and functions are protected, preventing accidental modification and promoting maintainability.
- **Reusability:** Modules can be used in multiple parts of your application or even shared across projects.
- **Namespace Management:** Modules help avoid naming collisions with other global variables or functions.
- **Clear Separation of Concerns:** Modules focus on specific tasks, leading to cleaner and more organized code.

The Module Pattern is a powerful tool in your JavaScript arsenal. By harnessing the power of closures, it empowers you to build modular, reusable, and well-structured code that scales gracefully as your projects grow. While modern JavaScript offers native modules (ES modules), understanding the Module Pattern deepens your grasp of closures and their practical applications.

Private Variables: Keeping Secrets with Closures

In JavaScript, the concept of truly private variables doesn't exist in the same way it does in languages like Java or C++. However, closures provide a clever workaround, allowing you to create variables that are effectively hidden from the outside world. This technique is essential for building robust and maintainable code.

The Power of Data Hiding

Data hiding, also known as encapsulation, is a fundamental principle of software engineering. It involves restricting access to certain parts of your code, specifically data (variables) and the functions that operate on that data (methods). The goal is to:

- **Prevent Accidental Modification:** Protect your data from being unintentionally changed by external code, leading to unpredictable behavior and bugs.
- **Maintain Code Integrity:** Ensure that data is accessed and modified only through a well-defined interface, making your code more reliable and easier to reason about.
- **Promote Modularity:** Break down your code into smaller, self-contained units (modules or objects) that are easier to understand, test, and maintain.

Closures as Guardians of Privacy

Closures play a crucial role in achieving data hiding in JavaScript. When you define a function inside another function, the inner function forms a closure. This closure encapsulates the variables declared in its outer function's scope, making them inaccessible to the outside world.

The Module Pattern Revisited: A Classic Example

The Module Pattern, discussed in the previous section, is a prime example of using closures to create private variables. Let's revisit our counter module:

```
const counterModule = (function() {
  let count = 0; // Private variable

  // ... (public API functions) ...
})();
```

The `count` variable is private because it's declared within the closure created by the IIFE. The only way to access or modify `count` is through the module's public API functions, ensuring controlled and predictable interactions.

The Revealing Module Pattern: A Variation

The Revealing Module Pattern is a slight variation of the Module Pattern that offers a more explicit way to define the public API.

```
const counterModule = (function() {
  let count = 0;

  function increment() { count++; }
  function decrement() { count--; }
  function getValue() { return count; }

  return {
    increment: increment,
    getValue: getValue
  }; // Only expose some functions
})();

counterModule.increment();
console.log(counterModule.getValue()); // Output: 1
```

Here, we explicitly list the functions we want to expose in the returned object, making the public API more apparent.

Other Closure-Based Patterns

Closures can be used in various patterns to achieve data hiding:

- **Private Methods:** You can create private methods within objects using closures.
- **Factory Functions:** These functions can create multiple objects, each with its own private data, using closures.
- **Singleton Pattern:** Closures can be used to implement the Singleton pattern, ensuring that only one instance of a class or object exists.

Key Takeaways

Closures are a powerful tool for data hiding and encapsulation in JavaScript. By creating private variables, you can protect your data from unintended modification, improve code maintainability, and promote modularity. The Module Pattern and the Revealing Module Pattern are two common ways to leverage closures for creating modules with private and public interfaces.

Event Handling: Closures and Persistent State

In the realm of interactive web applications, event handlers are your code's way of responding to user actions like clicks, hovers, or form submissions. But handling events isn't just about reacting in the moment; it's also about remembering the context in which those events occurred. This is where closures step in, acting as time capsules to preserve the state of variables.

The Challenge: Dynamically Changing Values

Imagine you're creating a series of buttons dynamically using JavaScript, each with a unique identifier. You want each button to display its ID when clicked. However, a straightforward approach can lead to unexpected results:

```
for (let i = 0; i < 3; i++) {
  let btn = document.createElement('button');
  btn.textContent = `Button ${i}`;
  btn.addEventListener('click', function() {
    console.log(`You clicked Button ${i}`);
  });
  document.body.appendChild(btn);
}
```

If you click any of the buttons, you might expect the console to log something like "You clicked Button 0," "You clicked Button 1," etc. However, it will always log "You clicked Button 3" for each button. This happens because the `i` variable is shared across all event handlers and its value changes with each iteration of the loop. By the time any button is clicked, `i` has already reached its final value of 3.

Closures to the Rescue: Preserving the Snapshot

To solve this issue, we need to capture the value of `i` at the time each event listener is created. This is where closures come into play.

```
for (let i = 0; i < 3; i++) {
  let btn = document.createElement('button');
  btn.textContent = `Button ${i}`;
  btn.addEventListener('click', (function(index) {
    return function() {
      console.log(`You clicked Button ${index}`);
    };
  })(i));
  document.body.appendChild(btn);
}
```

Let's break down how closures fix this:

1. **IIFE for Closure:** We wrap the event handler in an Immediately Invoked Function Expression (IIFE). This creates a new scope for each button, preventing variable `i` from being shared.
2. **Passing the State:** We pass the current value of `i` (renamed `index` for clarity) as an argument to the IIFE.
3. **Returning the Handler:** The IIFE returns a new function (the actual event handler) that has access to the `index` variable due to closure. This function is what's ultimately attached as the event listener.

Now, each event handler holds onto the value of `index` that was passed to it when it was created. When you click a button, the correct `index` value is logged.

Beyond Buttons: Remembering State

This pattern is not limited to buttons. You can use closures in event handlers to capture any relevant data at the time the event is attached. This allows your callbacks to operate with the correct context, even if the original data has changed later.

For instance, closures are essential for:

- **AJAX Requests:** Callbacks for handling responses can use closures to access data related to the original request.
- **Form Handling:** Submit event handlers can use closures to capture form field values before the form is reset.
- **Timers:** Closures can help you keep track of time or state between timer intervals.

Closures are a powerful tool in your JavaScript arsenal. By understanding how they preserve state, you can create more reliable and dynamic event handlers and unlock the full potential of asynchronous programming in JavaScript.

Common Closure Pitfalls: Memory Leaks and `this`

While closures are incredibly useful, they can also lead to subtle problems if not used with caution. Let's explore two common pitfalls and how to avoid them:

1. Memory Leaks: The Clingy Closure

Closures can inadvertently cause memory leaks in JavaScript. This happens when a closure holds a reference to an object that's no longer needed, preventing the garbage collector from reclaiming its memory.

```
function outerFunction() {
  let largeArray = new Array(1000000); // Large object

  return function() {
    console.log(largeArray[0]); // Closure references largeArray
  };
}

const myClosure = outerFunction();
// ... (largeArray is not used elsewhere but cannot be garbage collected)
```

In this example, the `myClosure` function holds a reference to `largeArray`. Even if `largeArray` is not used anywhere else, it cannot be garbage collected because the closure still needs it. This can lead to a significant memory leak over time.

Prevention:

- **Nulling Out References:** When you're done with the outer function, explicitly set any references to large objects within the closure to `null`.
- **Avoiding Circular References:** Be cautious of circular references, where an object references itself through a closure, as this can also prevent garbage collection.
- **Using Weak References:** In certain cases, you can use `WeakMap` or `WeakSet` to hold references to objects within closures. Weak references allow the garbage collector to reclaim objects if they are not referenced elsewhere.

2. `this` Binding Issues: The Shapeshifting Keyword

The `this` keyword can be unpredictable within closures, especially in event handlers. Since closures inherit the `this` value from their surrounding scope, it may not always be what you expect.

```
const obj = {
  name: "My Object",
  handleClick: function() {
    document.addEventListener("click", function() {
      console.log(this.name); // undefined (this refers to the event target)
    });
  }
};

obj.handleClick();
```

In this example, `this` within the event handler refers to the element that was clicked (the event target), not the `obj` object.

Solution: Arrow Functions

Arrow functions offer a straightforward solution to this problem. They don't have their own `this` binding; instead, they inherit `this` from the surrounding scope.

```
document.addEventListener("click", () => {
  console.log(this.name); // "My Object"
});
```

Best Practices for Avoiding Closure Pitfalls

- **Be Mindful of References:** Carefully manage references to objects within closures to prevent memory leaks.
- **Prefer Arrow Functions:** Use arrow functions in event handlers and callbacks to avoid issues with `this` binding.
- **Test Thoroughly:** Test your code in various scenarios to ensure that closures are not causing unexpected side effects.
- **Learn Advanced Techniques:** Explore techniques like WeakMaps and WeakSets for managing references within closures more efficiently.

By understanding these common pitfalls and applying best practices, you can leverage the power of closures while avoiding their potential drawbacks, ensuring that your JavaScript code remains robust and efficient.

Chapter Summary

In this chapter, we delved into the practical side of closures, exploring how they power modules, enable data privacy, and play a crucial role in event handling. We learned how the Module Pattern leverages closures to create encapsulated code with private and public interfaces, leading to more organized and maintainable codebases.

We also saw how closures enable the creation of private variables within functions and objects, promoting data hiding and ensuring that data is accessed and modified only through controlled channels. By preserving the state of variables at the time of their creation, closures play a vital role in event handlers, allowing callback functions to remember the context in which they were defined.

However, we also uncovered some potential pitfalls of closures, such as memory leaks and unexpected behavior with the `this` keyword. We discussed strategies to mitigate these issues, including nulling out references, using arrow functions for callbacks, and being mindful of how closures capture variables by reference.

By mastering closures and their practical applications, you have gained a valuable tool for building modular, maintainable, and robust JavaScript code. You are now equipped to create private variables, write stateful event handlers, and avoid common closure-related errors. This knowledge will be invaluable as you continue your journey to master JavaScript and tackle more complex development challenges.

Section IV:
Building Your Own JavaScript Tools

Constructing a Framework (Part 1): Core Principles and Structure

Outline

- What is a JavaScript Framework?
- Why Build Your Own Framework?
- Core Principles of Framework Design
- The Basic Structure of a JavaScript Framework
- Chapter Summary

What is a JavaScript Framework?

Imagine trying to build a house without a blueprint or any tools. It would be a daunting task, full of trial and error. That's where JavaScript frameworks come in. They provide a pre-built structure, like a blueprint, and a set of tools to streamline the process of building modern web applications.

What They Are

A JavaScript framework is a collection of pre-written JavaScript code, libraries, and conventions that help you build complex web applications more efficiently. They offer solutions to common development challenges, abstracting away many low-level details and allowing you to focus on the unique aspects of your application.

Common Features

Most JavaScript frameworks share several key features:

- **Data Binding:** This automatically synchronizes data between your application's model (data) and view (UI), making it easier to keep your interface updated when data changes.
- **Component-Based Architecture:** Frameworks encourage you to break down your UI into reusable components, each responsible for a specific part of the interface. This modular approach improves organization and maintainability.
- **Routing:** Routing allows you to define how your application should respond to different URLs, enabling smooth navigation and user experience.
- **State Management:** As your application grows in complexity, managing its state (the data that changes over time) becomes crucial. Frameworks provide tools or patterns to handle state changes efficiently.
- **Templating:** Frameworks often include templating engines that make it easier to generate dynamic HTML based on your data.
- **Testing Utilities:** Many frameworks offer built-in testing tools to ensure the quality and reliability of your code.

Benefits of Using Frameworks

- **Faster Development:** Frameworks provide pre-built components and structure, allowing you to build applications faster than starting from scratch.
- **Improved Code Organization:** Component-based architecture and other patterns promoted by frameworks help you write cleaner, more organized code.
- **Easier Maintenance:** Well-structured code is easier to maintain and update as your application evolves.
- **Community and Support:** Popular frameworks have large communities of developers, extensive documentation, and plenty of resources to help you overcome challenges.
- **Best Practices:** Frameworks often embody best practices for web development, leading to more robust and secure applications.

Popular JavaScript Frameworks

Some of the most popular JavaScript frameworks include:

- **React:** Developed by Facebook, known for its component-based architecture and virtual DOM.
- **Angular:** Developed by Google, a full-featured framework with a strong focus on structure and testability.
- **Vue.js:** A progressive framework known for its flexibility and ease of integration.

When to Use a Framework

Frameworks are ideal for building complex web applications that require:

- **Dynamic User Interfaces:** Frequent updates and interactions with the user.
- **Single-Page Applications (SPAs):** Applications that load once and update dynamically without full page reloads.
- **Large Codebases:** Projects where code organization and maintainability are critical.

Choosing the Right Framework

The best framework for you depends on your project requirements, team experience, and personal preferences. Experiment with different frameworks to find one that fits your needs and development style.

Why Build Your Own Framework?

While using an existing framework is often a practical choice, there are compelling reasons why you might embark on the journey of building your own custom JavaScript framework. This path is not for the faint of heart, but it offers unique benefits and opportunities for growth.

Deeper Understanding: Unveiling the Inner Workings

Building a framework from scratch is like dissecting a complex machine. You'll gain an intimate understanding of how the various components work together, how data flows through the system, and how rendering and updates are managed. This knowledge will make you a more proficient JavaScript developer and give you a deeper appreciation for the complexities of modern web applications.

Learning Experience: A Challenging Journey of Growth

Creating your own framework is a significant undertaking that will push your JavaScript skills to new heights. You'll encounter challenges and roadblocks that will force you to learn new techniques, design patterns, and architectural principles. The lessons you learn from this experience will be invaluable as you tackle other complex projects in the future.

Tailored Solutions: Crafting Your Perfect Tool

Existing frameworks are designed to be general-purpose solutions. They often include features that you might not need, adding bloat to your application. By building your own framework, you can tailor it precisely to your specific requirements, resulting in a leaner, more efficient codebase. You have the freedom to choose the features you want, implement them in the way that makes the most sense for your project, and avoid unnecessary overhead.

Creativity and Innovation: Breaking New Ground

Building a framework gives you the opportunity to experiment and explore new ideas. You can try out innovative approaches to data binding, component management, or state management. You can challenge existing conventions and potentially discover new and better ways to solve common problems in web development. Who knows, your custom framework might even become the next big thing in the JavaScript world!

A Word of Caution: Not Always Practical

While building your own framework can be a valuable learning experience, it's not always the most practical choice for every project. If you have tight deadlines or limited resources, using an established framework might be a more sensible approach. However, if you have the time and curiosity, building your own framework can be a rewarding adventure that will take your JavaScript expertise to the next level.

Core Principles of Framework Design

Before diving into the actual implementation of your JavaScript framework, it's crucial to establish a solid foundation based on core design principles. These principles will guide your decisions throughout the development process, ensuring that your framework is well-structured, maintainable, and scalable.

Modularity: The Power of Small, Reusable Pieces

A modular approach is essential when building a framework. It involves breaking down the framework into smaller, independent modules, each responsible for a specific task or set of related tasks. This approach offers several benefits:

- **Organization:** Code is easier to understand and manage when it's divided into smaller, focused modules.
- **Reusability:** Modules can be reused in different parts of the framework or even in other projects, saving you time and effort.
- **Maintainability:** Changes to one module are less likely to impact other parts of the framework, making updates and bug fixes easier.

For example, your framework might have separate modules for handling data fetching, routing, component rendering, and state management.

Separation of Concerns: Dividing and Conquering

Separation of Concerns (SoC) is a design principle that advocates for dividing a complex system into distinct parts, each with its own specific responsibility. In the context of a JavaScript framework, this means separating the concerns of data handling, UI rendering, and application logic.

- **Data Layer:** This layer handles fetching, storing, and manipulating data. It might interact with APIs or databases.
- **View Layer:** This layer focuses on rendering the user interface based on the data and handling user interactions.

- **Controller/Logic Layer:** This layer contains the business logic of your application, making decisions based on data and user input, and orchestrating communication between the data and view layers.

By adhering to SoC, you create a more modular and maintainable framework, where each layer can be developed and tested independently.

Extensibility: Future-Proof Your Framework

A well-designed framework should be extensible, allowing developers to customize and add features without modifying the core code. This is achieved through hooks or APIs that provide entry points for external code to interact with the framework.

Think of hooks as pre-defined places in your framework's code where custom functions can be "hooked in" to modify behavior or add new functionality. For example, you could have hooks for:

- **Component Lifecycle Events:** Functions that are executed when a component is created, updated, or destroyed.
- **Data Validation:** Functions that validate user input or data received from an API.
- **Custom Rendering:** Functions that allow developers to create their own UI elements or override the default rendering behavior.

Testability: Building with Confidence

Writing testable code is essential for ensuring the reliability and robustness of your framework. A testable framework is easier to debug, maintain, and extend.

Consider these practices:

- **Dependency Injection:** Use dependency injection to make your modules less tightly coupled, enabling easier testing in isolation.
- **Unit Testing:** Write unit tests to verify the behavior of individual modules and functions.
- **Integration Testing:** Write integration tests to ensure that different modules work together seamlessly.

Performance: Speed and Efficiency

In the world of web applications, performance is paramount. A slow or unresponsive application can lead to frustrated users and lost business. When designing your framework, consider performance optimizations like:

- **Minimizing DOM Manipulation:** Direct manipulation of the Document Object Model (DOM) can be expensive. Use techniques like virtual DOM diffing to minimize the number of actual DOM updates.
- **Efficient Algorithms:** Choose efficient algorithms and data structures to handle data processing and rendering.
- **Lazy Loading:** Load resources (like images or scripts) only when they are needed to improve initial load time.
- **Caching:** Cache data or calculated results to avoid redundant computations.

By adhering to these core principles of framework design, you'll lay a strong foundation for creating a JavaScript framework that is not only functional but also maintainable, extensible, and performant.

The Basic Structure of a JavaScript Framework

A JavaScript framework, like any complex system, is built upon a set of interconnected components. Understanding this basic structure provides a roadmap for your framework development journey.

Data Layer: The Source of Truth

The data layer is responsible for managing the data that powers your application. It handles:

- **Data Retrieval:** Fetching data from external sources, such as APIs or databases.
- **Data Storage:** Storing data locally or in a central repository.
- **Data Manipulation:** Transforming, filtering, and aggregating data for use in your application.

In your framework, you might create a data module that encapsulates these operations, providing a clean API for interacting with data.

View Layer: Painting the Picture

The view layer is the visual representation of your application. It's responsible for:

- **Rendering:** Translating data into HTML elements and displaying them on the screen.
- **User Interaction:** Handling user events like clicks, form submissions, and other interactions.

Your framework's view layer might include a templating engine or component system to define how data is displayed and how components interact with each other.

Controller/Logic Layer: The Decision-Maker

The controller or logic layer is the brain of your application. It handles:

- **Business Logic:** The rules and processes that define how your application behaves.
- **Mediation:** It receives user input from the view layer, fetches and updates data from the data layer, and instructs the view layer to update the UI accordingly.

In your framework, the controller layer might be implemented as a set of functions or classes that manage the flow of data and logic within your application.

Routing: Mapping URLs to Views

Routing is the mechanism that determines which view or component to display based on the current URL. It's like a map that guides users through your application.

Your framework's routing system might use regular expressions or pattern matching to map URLs to specific views or components. When the URL changes, the router updates the view layer to display the appropriate content.

A Simplified Example

Let's consider a simple blog application built with your framework:

```
// Data Layer (simplified)
const posts = [
  { id: 1, title: "Post 1", content: "..." },
  { id: 2, title: "Post 2", content: "..." }
];

// View Layer (simplified)
function renderPost(post) {
  // ... (code to render the post's title and content) ...
}

// Controller/Logic Layer (simplified)
```

```
function showPost(postId) {
  const post = posts.find(post => post.id === postId);
  renderPost(post);
}

// Routing (simplified)
const routes = {
  "/posts/:id": showPost // Route for individual posts
};

// ... (code to match the current URL to a route and call the corresponding
function) …
```

The Iterative Process of Framework Building

Building a JavaScript framework is not a one-time task; it's an ongoing process of refinement and improvement. You'll start with a basic structure, implement core features, and then iteratively add more functionality, optimize performance, and test your framework in various scenarios.

This chapter has laid the groundwork by introducing the fundamental components and principles of framework design. In the following chapters, we'll delve deeper into each of these components, providing more detailed guidance and examples to help you craft your own custom JavaScript framework.

Chapter Summary

In this chapter, we laid the foundation for constructing your own JavaScript framework. We explored the concept of a framework as a pre-built structure and set of tools that streamline web application development. We discussed the motivations for building a custom framework, including gaining a deeper understanding of how frameworks work, personal learning, and the ability to create tailored solutions.

We also delved into the core principles that guide framework design, emphasizing modularity, separation of concerns, extensibility, testability, and performance. These principles serve as the guiding lights for creating a robust, maintainable, and scalable framework.

Finally, we outlined the basic structure of a JavaScript framework, introducing the key components: the data layer, view layer, controller/logic layer, and routing. We provided a simplified example to illustrate how these components interact in a basic application.

This chapter has set the stage for your journey into framework development. In the following chapters, we'll delve deeper into each of these components, providing more detailed guidance and examples. Remember, building a framework is an iterative process. Start with the basics, experiment, and refine your code as you learn and grow.

Constructing a Framework (Part 2): Routing, Components, and Templating

Outline

- Routing: Navigating Your Application
- Components: Building Blocks of the UI
- Templating: Dynamic Content Generation
- String-Based Templates: Simple but Limited
- Template Literals: JavaScript's Built-in Templates
- Templating Libraries: Advanced Features
- Chapter Summary

Routing: Navigating Your Application

In the world of web applications, routing is the GPS that guides users to their desired destinations. It's the mechanism that determines which part of your application to display based on the current URL. Just like a road map helps you navigate a city, routing helps users explore your web app by associating specific URLs with corresponding views or components.

How Routing Works

Routing involves several key elements:

1. **URLs:** The addresses that users type into their browser to access different parts of your application.
2. **Routes:** The definitions that map specific URLs to corresponding views or components.
3. **Router:** The component or module responsible for matching the current URL to a defined route and rendering the associated content.

When a user clicks a link or types a URL into the browser, the router intercepts the request, checks the URL, and determines which view or component to display. This process allows users to navigate seamlessly between different sections of your application.

Types of Routing

There are two main types of routing in JavaScript:

1. **Hash-Based Routing:** This older method uses the hash fragment (#) in the URL to manage routing. For example, `http://mywebsite.com/#/about` might display the "About" page. Hash-based routing is simple to implement but has some limitations, such as less clean URLs and potential issues with browser history.
2. **History API Routing:** This newer method leverages the HTML5 History API, which provides a cleaner and more robust way to manage routing. URLs look more natural (e.g., `http://mywebsite.com/about`), and you can use the browser's back and forward buttons seamlessly. However, it requires server-side configuration to handle initial page loads correctly.

Building a Simple Router

You can create a basic router in your framework using conditional statements and event listeners:

```
const routes = {
  "/": homeComponent,
  "/about": aboutComponent,
  "/contact": contactComponent
};

function navigate(path) {
  if (routes[path]) {
    const component = routes[path];
    // ... (code to render the component) ...
  } else {
    // ... (handle 404 Not Found errors) ...
  }
}

window.addEventListener("popstate", () => {
  navigate(window.location.pathname);
});
```

In this example:

1. `routes` is an object that maps URLs to components.
2. `navigate` is a function that renders the appropriate component based on the `path`.
3. An event listener is added to the `popstate` event, which is triggered when the user navigates using the browser's back or forward buttons. This calls `navigate` to update the view accordingly.

Evolving Your Router

This is a very simplified example. As your framework grows, you'll likely need to add more features to your router, such as:

- **Route Parameters:** To capture dynamic values within URLs (e.g., `/users/123`).
- **Nested Routes:** To support hierarchical navigation structures.
- **Guards:** To control access to certain routes based on user authentication or permissions.
- **Transitions and Animations:** To create smooth visual transitions between views.

However, even with these basic building blocks, you can start creating a functional routing system within your custom framework.

Components: Building Blocks of the UI

Components are the fundamental building blocks of modern web applications. They encapsulate the structure, logic, and styling of specific parts of the user interface, making them reusable and easier to maintain. By promoting modularity, components enable developers to break down complex UIs into manageable, self-contained pieces. This approach enhances the development process by allowing individual components to be developed, tested, and debugged independently.

Types of Components

In JavaScript frameworks like React, components can be broadly classified into two types:

1. **Functional Components**: These are simpler and primarily concerned with rendering the UI. They are written as JavaScript functions and can accept props (properties) to customize their output. With the introduction of React Hooks, functional components can also manage state and side effects, making them even more powerful.

2. **Class Components**: These components are ES6 classes that extend from `React.Component`. They can hold and manage their state and lifecycle methods, providing more control over the component's behavior and rendering.

Functional Components

Functional components are typically used when the component's primary responsibility is to render some UI based on the props it receives. Here's an example of a simple functional component:

```
import React from 'react';

function Greeting(props) {
  return <h1>Hello, {props.name}!</h1>;
}

export default Greeting;
```

In this example, the `Greeting` component takes a `name` prop and renders a greeting message. It's a stateless component since it doesn't manage any internal state.

Class Components

Class components are used when more functionality is needed, such as managing internal state or utilizing lifecycle methods. Here's an example of a class component:

```
import React, { Component } from 'react';

class Counter extends Component {
  constructor(props) {
    super(props);
    this.state = { count: 0 };
  }

  increment = () => {
    this.setState({ count: this.state.count + 1 });
  }

  render() {
    return (
      <div>
        <p>Count: {this.state.count}</p>
        <button onClick={this.increment}>Increment</button>
      </div>
    );
  }
}

export default Counter;
```

In this example, the `Counter` component manages its own state (`count`) and provides a method (`increment`) to update that state. The component re-renders whenever the state changes, reflecting the updated count.

Promoting Modularity and Reusability

By using components, developers can achieve a high degree of modularity and reusability in their code. Components can be composed together to build more complex UIs. They can also be shared across different parts of an application or even across different projects, making development faster and more efficient.

In summary, components are the building blocks of modern web UIs, providing a structured way to build, maintain, and reuse UI elements. Whether using functional components for simplicity or class components for more control, understanding how to create and manage components is essential for any web developer.

Templating: Dynamic Content Generation

Templating is a powerful technique in web development that allows you to generate dynamic HTML content based on data. Instead of manually constructing HTML strings with variables and concatenation, templates provide a structured and more maintainable way to define the layout and structure of your UI elements.

Why Use Templates?

- **Separation of Concerns:** Templates help separate presentation logic (how data is displayed) from application logic (how data is fetched and manipulated). This makes your code cleaner, easier to understand, and more testable.
- **Reusability:** Templates can be reused to render different sets of data, reducing code duplication.
- **Maintainability:** Changes to the UI structure or styling can be made in one place (the template), rather than scattered throughout your code.
- **Dynamic Content:** Templates allow you to easily inject dynamic data into your HTML, creating interactive and personalized experiences.

Templating Approaches: From Simple to Sophisticated

JavaScript offers various templating approaches, each with its own advantages and trade-offs:

1. String-Based Templates:

String-based templates involve embedding variables and expressions directly within HTML strings using concatenation or string interpolation.

```
const name = "Alice";
const greeting = `<h1>Hello, ${name}!</h1>`;
```

While simple to use, this approach can become unwieldy for complex templates and might introduce security vulnerabilities (e.g., cross-site scripting) if not handled carefully.

2. Template Literals (ES6+):

Template literals, introduced in ES6, offer a more elegant way to embed expressions within strings using the backtick (`) syntax.

```
const product = { name: "Laptop", price: 999.99 };
const template = `
  <div class="product">
    <h2>${product.name}</h2>
    <p>Price: $${product.price}</p>
  </div>
`;
```

Template literals support multi-line strings, variable interpolation, and even expressions, making them a convenient choice for simple templating needs.

3. Templating Libraries:

For more complex applications, dedicated templating libraries like Handlebars or Mustache offer additional features:

- **Loops and Conditionals:** Easily iterate over arrays or conditionally render content.
- **Partial Templates:** Reuse smaller templates within larger ones.
- **Helpers:** Custom functions for formatting data or performing calculations within templates.

```
// Using Handlebars (example)
const template =
Handlebars.compile("<h1>{{title}}</h1><p>{{content}}</p>");
const data = { title: "My Blog Post", content: "This is my blog post
content." };
const html = template(data);
```

Rendering Templates: Bringing Them to Life

To render a template, you typically combine the template string with your data and insert the resulting HTML into the DOM. This process can be done manually or with the help of libraries or frameworks that provide more sophisticated rendering mechanisms.

Key Takeaways

Templating is a powerful tool that enables dynamic content generation and improves the organization and maintainability of your web applications. By choosing the right templating approach (string-based, template literals, or libraries) and carefully managing your data, you can create engaging and interactive user interfaces with ease.

String-Based Templates: Simple but Limited

String-based templates represent the simplest form of templating in JavaScript. They involve combining plain strings with variables and expressions to dynamically generate HTML content.

Concatenation: The Old-School Way

In the earlier days of JavaScript, developers used string concatenation to create templates:

```
const name = "Alice";
const greeting = "<h1>Hello, " + name + "!</h1>";
```

Here, the + operator is used to concatenate the string literals (`"<h1>Hello, "`, `"!"`, and `"</h1>"`) with the variable `name`. While this approach works, it can quickly become messy and difficult to read, especially with more complex templates.

String Interpolation: A Modern Twist

Modern JavaScript (ES6+) introduced template literals (backticks `), which offer a more convenient way to embed variables and expressions within strings:

```
const product = { name: "Laptop", price: 999.99 };
const template = `
  <div class="product">
```

```
    <h2>${product.name}</h2>
    <p>Price: $${product.price}</p>
  </div>
`;
```

In this example, the `${product.name}` and `${product.price}` expressions are evaluated and inserted into the string, resulting in a dynamic HTML template.

Limitations of String-Based Templates

While string-based templates are easy to understand and use, they have some drawbacks:

1. **Readability:** Complex templates can become hard to read and maintain due to the mix of HTML, variables, and expressions.
2. **Security Risks:** Directly inserting user-generated content into templates can lead to vulnerabilities like cross-site scripting (XSS) attacks. It's crucial to sanitize or escape user input to mitigate these risks.
3. **Limited Features:** String-based templates lack the advanced features provided by dedicated templating libraries, such as loops, conditionals, and inheritance.
4. **No Separation of Logic:** The mixing of HTML and JavaScript code can make it harder to separate presentation logic from application logic, hindering maintainability.

When to Use String-Based Templates

String-based templates can still be useful in scenarios where you need to quickly generate simple dynamic content and the potential limitations are not a major concern. For example, they might be suitable for:

- Small, self-contained components.
- Prototyping or simple applications.
- Situations where you have full control over the input data and security is not a major concern.

However, for larger and more complex applications, it's generally recommended to use dedicated templating libraries like Handlebars or Mustache, which offer more powerful features, better readability, and enhanced security.

Template Literals: JavaScript's Built-in Templates

Template literals, introduced in ES6 (ECMAScript 2015), offer a significant upgrade to JavaScript's string handling capabilities. They provide a concise and expressive way to create templates directly within your JavaScript code, eliminating the need for cumbersome string concatenation.

The Backtick Syntax: Unleashing Expression Power

Unlike traditional strings delimited by single or double quotes, template literals use backticks (`` ` ``). This seemingly minor change unlocks a world of possibilities:

1. **Expression Interpolation:** You can embed JavaScript expressions directly within your template literals using `${...}`. These expressions are evaluated and their results are inserted into the resulting string.

   ```
   const name = "Alice";
   const age = 30;
   const greeting = `Hello, ${name}! You are ${age} years old.`;
   console.log(greeting); // Output: "Hello, Alice! You are 30 years old."
   ```

2. **Multi-line Strings:** Template literals make it effortless to create multi-line strings without the need for escape characters or cumbersome concatenation.

   ```
   const message = `This is a
   multi-line
   string.`;
   ```

3. **Nested Templates:** You can even nest template literals within each other for greater flexibility.

   ```
   const outer = `Outer template: ${`Inner template: ${name}`}`;
   ```

Enhanced Readability and Maintainability

Template literals significantly improve the readability and maintainability of your code. The ability to embed expressions directly within the template eliminates the need for awkward string concatenation and makes your code easier to understand.

```
const product = { name: "Laptop", price: 999.99 };
const template = `
  <div class="product">
    <h2>${product.name}</h2>
    <p>Price: $${product.price}</p>
  </div>
`;
```

Practical Applications

Template literals are versatile and can be used in various scenarios:

- **Dynamic HTML Generation:** Create HTML templates that can be populated with data from your JavaScript code.
- **Formatted Output:** Easily generate strings with formatted numbers, dates, and other data types.
- **Localization:** Create multilingual applications by embedding localized strings within templates.
- **SQL Queries:** Construct dynamic SQL queries with variable substitution.

Key Takeaways

Template literals are a powerful and convenient tool for working with strings and creating templates in JavaScript. They offer a more readable and maintainable way to embed expressions within strings, support multi-line strings, and enable dynamic content generation. By mastering template literals, you can write cleaner, more expressive code and unlock new possibilities for building dynamic user interfaces and applications.

While template literals are a great built-in option for many templating needs, remember that dedicated libraries like Handlebars or Mustache offer even more advanced features, such as conditional rendering and loops, which we'll explore in the next section of this chapter.

Templating Libraries: Advanced Features

While template literals are convenient for basic templating, dedicated libraries like Handlebars or Mustache offer a wealth of features that make managing complex user interfaces a breeze. Let's explore why these libraries are essential for your framework.

Why Use Templating Libraries?

1. **Advanced Features:**

- **Loops:** Iterate over arrays or objects to generate repetitive HTML structures (e.g., lists, tables).
- **Conditionals:** Render different content based on logical conditions, creating dynamic and personalized views.
- **Partial Templates:** Reuse smaller templates within larger ones to avoid code duplication and improve maintainability.
- **Inheritance:** Create template hierarchies, where child templates inherit and extend the structure of parent templates.
- **Custom Helpers:** Define your own functions to perform formatting, calculations, or other logic within templates.

2. **Clear Separation of Logic:**

   Templating libraries enforce a clear separation between your application's data and the presentation logic. This makes your code more organized, easier to test, and less prone to errors.

3. **Performance Optimizations:**

   Many libraries offer performance optimizations like pre-compilation, caching, and efficient DOM manipulation techniques, leading to faster rendering and smoother user experiences.

Popular Templating Libraries: Handlebars and Mustache

- **Handlebars:** A powerful and flexible library with a rich feature set, including loops, conditionals, helpers, and partials. It allows you to create complex templates with ease.
- **Mustache:** A simpler library with a more minimalist approach. It focuses on logic-less templates, which can improve readability and maintainability.

Integrating a Library into Your Framework

To integrate a templating library into your framework, follow these general steps:

1. **Include the Library:** Add the library's JavaScript file to your project. You can download it from the library's website or use a package manager like npm.
2. **Create Templates:** Define your templates using the library's syntax. For example, in Handlebars, you might use double curly braces `{{...}}` for variables and expressions.
3. **Compile Templates (if necessary):** Some libraries require you to compile templates into functions before you can use them.
4. **Render Templates:** Pass your data to the compiled template function, and the library will generate the corresponding HTML string.
5. **Insert into DOM:** Insert the generated HTML into the appropriate place in your application's Document Object Model (DOM).

Example: Using Handlebars

```
// Assuming you have included Handlebars in your project
const templateString = `
  <ul>
    {{#each items}}
      <li>{{name}} - ${{price}}</li>
    {{/each}}
  </ul>
`;

const template = Handlebars.compile(templateString);
const data = { items: [{ name: "Item 1", price: 10 }, { name: "Item 2", price:
20 }] };
const html = template(data);
```

```
document.body.innerHTML = html;
```

In this example:

- We define a Handlebars template with a loop (`#each`) to iterate over the `items` array.
- We compile the template into a function using `Handlebars.compile()`.
- We pass the `data` object to the compiled template, which generates the HTML list.
- We insert the generated HTML into the `body` of the document.

By leveraging templating libraries, you can create more complex and dynamic user interfaces in your JavaScript framework. These libraries offer a wide range of features that streamline template creation and rendering, making your code more maintainable and your UI more engaging.

Chapter Summary

In this chapter, we delved deeper into the essential components of building a JavaScript framework. We explored the concept of routing, the mechanism that maps URLs to specific views or components, enabling seamless navigation within your web application. We discussed different routing approaches, from simple hash-based routing to the more advanced History API routing.

Next, we introduced the concept of components as reusable building blocks that encapsulate UI structure, logic, and styling. We learned how components promote modularity, reusability, and maintainability in your framework.

Finally, we explored templating, a powerful technique for generating dynamic HTML content based on data. We covered different templating approaches, ranging from basic string-based templates and template literals to the more sophisticated capabilities of dedicated templating libraries like Handlebars and Mustache.

With the knowledge gained in this chapter, you are now equipped to implement routing, build reusable components, and create dynamic user interfaces using templates in your custom JavaScript framework. This sets the stage for developing more complex and interactive web applications. In the next chapter, we will explore advanced framework concepts such as data binding, virtual DOM, and state management, further expanding your framework's capabilities.

Advanced Framework Concepts: Data Binding, Virtual DOM, and State Management

Outline

- Data Binding: Synchronizing Data and UI
- Virtual DOM: Efficient UI Updates
- State Management: The Heart of Dynamic Applications
- Chapter Summary

Data Binding: Synchronizing Data and UI

Data binding is the magical bridge that connects your application's underlying data (the model) with the elements of your user interface (the view). It creates a synchronized relationship where changes to one side are automatically reflected on the other, resulting in a dynamic and responsive user experience.

Two-Way Street: Data Changes Update UI, UI Actions Update Data

Think of data binding as a two-way street:

1. **Data to UI (Model to View):** When data in your application's model changes, the framework automatically updates the corresponding elements in the UI to reflect those changes. This ensures that what the user sees is always consistent with the underlying data.
2. **UI to Data (View to Model):** When users interact with UI elements (e.g., typing in an input field, clicking a button), these actions can trigger events that update the data model. The framework detects these changes and propagates them back to the view, keeping everything in sync.

Types of Data Binding: One-Way, Two-Way, and Events

1. **One-Way Binding:** Data flows in one direction, from the model to the view. Changes to the model update the UI, but UI interactions do not directly modify the data. This is often used for displaying data that doesn't need to be edited by the user.
2. **Two-Way Binding:** Data flows in both directions. Changes to the model update the UI, and changes in the UI update the model. This is common for interactive elements like input fields or forms.
3. **Event Binding:** UI events (clicks, hovers, etc.) are bound to functions in your code. These functions can then trigger updates to the data model.

Implementing Data Binding in Your Framework

There are several ways to implement data binding in your framework:

- **Dirty Checking:** Periodically checking the data model for changes and updating the UI accordingly.
- **Pub/Sub (Publish/Subscribe):** Using an event system to notify the UI of data changes.
- **Object.defineProperty() or Proxies:** Using JavaScript's property mechanisms to intercept changes to data properties and trigger UI updates.

The choice of implementation depends on your framework's design and performance considerations.

Example: Two-Way Data Binding

```
// Simplified example
```

```
const data = { message: "Hello" };
const inputElement = document.getElementById("myInput");
const displayElement = document.getElementById("myDisplay");

inputElement.value = data.message;
displayElement.textContent = data.message;

inputElement.addEventListener("input", function() {
  data.message = this.value;
  displayElement.textContent = this.value;
});
```

In this basic example, the `inputElement` and `displayElement` are bound to the `message` property of the `data` object. Changes to the input field update the data and the display element, while changes to the data (if made elsewhere in the code) would also update both UI elements.

The Power of Data Binding

Data binding is a core feature of many modern JavaScript frameworks. It simplifies the development of dynamic user interfaces, reduces boilerplate code, and makes your code easier to reason about by establishing a clear connection between data and UI elements. As you build your own framework, consider how you can implement data binding to make your applications more interactive and responsive.

Data Binding Implementations: Event Listeners, Property Descriptors, and Proxies

Let's delve into the practical implementation of data binding within your JavaScript framework using different techniques.

1. Event Listeners: The Reactive Approach

One common approach is to use event listeners to detect changes in your data model and update the UI accordingly. This approach is reactive, meaning it responds to events as they occur.

```
const data = { message: "Hello" };
const inputElement = document.getElementById("myInput");
const displayElement = document.getElementById("myDisplay");

function updateUI() {
  inputElement.value = data.message;
  displayElement.textContent = data.message;
}

// Initial UI update
updateUI();

Object.keys(data).forEach(key => {
  // Add event listeners to data properties
  Object.defineProperty(data, key, {
    set(newValue) {
      this["_" + key] = newValue; // Store actual value
      updateUI();                 // Update UI on change
    },
    get() {
      return this["_" + key];   // Retrieve actual value
    }
```

```
  });
});
```

In this example, we define an `updateUi` function that sets the input field value to the message and the text content to the message. We use `Object.defineProperty` to define setters and getters to update the UI whenever the data changes. We also call the `updateUI` function initially when we create the data object.

2. Property Descriptors: Fine-Grained Control

JavaScript's `Object.defineProperty()` method allows you to define custom property descriptors, including getter and setter functions. These functions can be used to intercept property access and trigger UI updates when data changes.

```
// Inside your framework's data binding module
function bindData(data, element, property) {
  Object.defineProperty(data, property, {
    set: function(newValue) {
      this["_" + property] = newValue;
      element.textContent = newValue;
    },
    get: function() {
      return this["_" + property];
    }
  });
}
```

The `bindData` function sets up a setter and getter for the specified property. The setter updates both the underlying data and the corresponding UI element. The getter retrieves the actual value.

3. Proxy Objects: The Interceptor

Proxy objects offer a more powerful and flexible way to intercept property access and modifications. They allow you to define custom behavior for a wide range of operations, including getting, setting, and deleting properties.

```
// Inside your framework's data binding module
function bindData(data, element, property) {
  const proxy = new Proxy(data, {
    set: function(target, prop, value) {
      target[prop] = value;
      element.textContent = value;
      return true; // Indicate success
    }
  });
  return proxy;
}
```

In this example, the `bindData` function creates a proxy object that traps property assignments and updates the UI element accordingly.

Choosing the Right Approach

Each data binding method has its own advantages and trade-offs:

- **Event Listeners:** Simple to implement for basic scenarios.

- **Property Descriptors:** Offer fine-grained control over individual properties.
- **Proxies:** Provide the most flexibility for complex data binding scenarios.

The best approach depends on the complexity of your framework and the specific requirements of your application.

Virtual DOM: Efficient UI Updates

Directly manipulating the Document Object Model (DOM) in JavaScript can be computationally expensive, especially in applications with frequent updates. The Virtual DOM (VDOM) is a clever technique that addresses this performance bottleneck by introducing a lightweight, in-memory representation of the actual DOM.

The VDOM as an Intermediary

Think of the VDOM as a blueprint or a virtual copy of your UI. It's a tree-like data structure that mirrors the structure of your actual DOM, but it's much simpler and faster to work with.

When your application data changes, instead of immediately updating the real DOM, the framework first updates the VDOM. This update is incredibly fast because it happens entirely in memory. Once the VDOM is updated, the framework performs a process called "diffing."

Diffing: The Key to Efficiency

Diffing involves comparing the new VDOM with the previous VDOM to identify the specific changes that need to be made to the actual DOM. This comparison algorithm is designed to be highly efficient, finding the minimal set of changes required to bring the real DOM in sync with the VDOM.

Once the differences are identified, the framework applies only those necessary changes to the actual DOM. This targeted approach significantly reduces the amount of direct DOM manipulation, which is often the main cause of performance issues in web applications.

Benefits of the Virtual DOM

- **Performance:** By minimizing direct DOM manipulation, the VDOM can drastically improve the performance of your application, especially for complex and dynamic UIs.
- **Abstraction:** The VDOM provides an abstraction layer between your application's data and the UI, making it easier to manage and reason about UI updates.
- **Cross-Platform Compatibility:** VDOMs are not tied to the browser environment and can be used to render UI on different platforms, like mobile devices or even server-side rendering.

Implementing a VDOM

The specific implementation details of a VDOM can vary depending on the framework you're building. However, the general concept remains the same:

1. **Create a Virtual Representation:** Represent your UI components and their state as lightweight JavaScript objects (nodes) in a tree-like structure.
2. **Update the VDOM:** When data changes, update the corresponding nodes in the VDOM.
3. **Diff:** Compare the new VDOM with the previous VDOM to identify changes.
4. **Patch:** Apply the minimum necessary changes to the actual DOM to match the new VDOM.

VDOM Libraries

Many JavaScript libraries and frameworks already provide VDOM implementations, such as React's Virtual DOM. You can leverage these libraries within your custom framework or draw inspiration from their implementation details.

Key Takeaway

The virtual DOM is a powerful technique for optimizing UI updates in JavaScript frameworks. By minimizing direct DOM manipulation and applying targeted changes, it significantly improves performance and responsiveness, making your web applications smoother and more enjoyable for users. As you continue building your framework, consider how you can incorporate a VDOM to enhance its capabilities.

Creating and Updating a Virtual DOM Representation

Let's illustrate a simplified example of how a virtual DOM representation could be created and updated for a basic component within your framework:

Core Concept

The VDOM is essentially a tree of plain JavaScript objects (nodes) that mirror the structure of your HTML. Each node describes an element, its attributes, and its children (which are also nodes).

Example: A "Greeting" Component

```
// Virtual DOM Node Representation
function createElement(type, props, ...children) {
  return {
    type,
    props: props || {},
    children: children.flat(), // Flatten nested arrays (if any)
  };
}

// Initial VDOM
const initialVDOM = createElement('div', { class: 'greeting' },
  createElement('h2', null, 'Hello'),
  createElement('p', null, 'Welcome to our website!')
);

// Updated VDOM (e.g., after data change)
const updatedVDOM = createElement('div', { class: 'greeting' },
  createElement('h2', null, 'Greetings'), // Updated heading
  createElement('p', null, 'We hope you enjoy your stay!') // Updated content
);

// (Simplified) Diffing Function
function diff(oldNode, newNode) {
  if (oldNode.type !== newNode.type) {
    // Replace the entire node if the type changed
    oldNode.elm.replaceWith(render(newNode));
  } else {
    // Update attributes
    for (const attr in newNode.props) {
      oldNode.elm.setAttribute(attr, newNode.props[attr]);
    }

    // Update children recursively
    const oldChildren = oldNode.children;
    const newChildren = newNode.children;
    for (let i = 0; i < newChildren.length; i++) {
```

```
        diff(oldChildren[i], newChildren[i]);
      }

      // Remove extra old children
      for (let i = newChildren.length; i < oldChildren.length; i++) {
        oldChildren[i].elm.remove();
      }
    }
}

// (Simplified) Rendering Function
function render(vNode) {
  const elm = document.createElement(vNode.type);
  for (const attr in vNode.props) {
    elm.setAttribute(attr, vNode.props[attr]);
  }
  vNode.children.forEach(child => elm.appendChild(render(child)));
  vNode.elm = elm; // Store a reference to the DOM element for efficient diffing
  return elm;
}
```

Explanation

1. **createElement:** This helper function constructs VDOM nodes as plain objects.
2. **initialVDOM & updatedVDOM:** These represent the component's state at different points in time.
3. **diff:** A simplified diffing function that compares nodes and their attributes recursively. If a node's type changes, it's replaced. Otherwise, attributes and child nodes are updated as needed.
4. **render:** This function turns a VDOM node into an actual DOM element. It recursively renders child nodes and attaches them.

How to Use It

1. Initially, you'd call `render(initialVDOM)` and append the resulting DOM element to the page.
2. When the component's data changes, create the `updatedVDOM`.
3. Call `diff(initialVDOM, updatedVDOM)` to figure out the minimal changes.
4. The `diff` function will modify the real DOM elements based on the comparison, resulting in an efficient update.

Important Considerations

- This is a simplified illustration. Real VDOM implementations in frameworks like React are far more sophisticated, handling more complex scenarios like component lifecycles, event handling, and optimizations.
- The goal of this example is to give you a conceptual understanding of how a VDOM represents UI elements and how diffing minimizes DOM manipulation for better performance.

State Management: The Heart of Dynamic Applications

As your JavaScript applications grow in complexity, managing the state – the data that changes over time – becomes a significant challenge. Without a well-organized approach, state management can quickly become a tangled web of scattered variables and unpredictable updates.

The Importance of State Management

State management is crucial for several reasons:

- **Data Consistency:** It ensures that different components of your application are always working with the latest and correct data, preventing inconsistencies and errors.
- **Data Sharing:** It provides a mechanism for sharing data between components, eliminating the need for complex prop drilling (passing data down through multiple levels of nested components).
- **Predictability:** It makes state changes more predictable and traceable, making your application easier to debug and maintain.
- **Performance:** Efficient state management can improve performance by minimizing unnecessary re-renders and optimizing updates to the user interface.

State Management Approaches: A Spectrum of Choices

There are various approaches to state management in JavaScript, each with its own strengths and weaknesses:

1. Local Component State: Small-Scale Simplicity

For simple components, managing state locally is often sufficient. You can use variables or object properties to store the component's internal state. When the state changes, the component re-renders itself to reflect the updates.

```
class Counter extends Component {
  constructor() {
    super();
    this.state = { count: 0 };
  }

  increment() {
    this.setState({ count: this.state.count + 1 });
  }

  render() {
    return `
      <p>Count: ${this.state.count}</p>
      <button onclick="${this.increment.bind(this)}">Increment</button>
    `;
  }
}
```

2. Global State Management: The Centralized Hub

As your application grows, managing state within individual components can become unwieldy. Global state management provides a centralized store for your application's data, making it accessible to all components.

Popular libraries like Redux and MobX offer sophisticated tools for global state management. They provide a single source of truth for your data, manage state changes through actions and reducers (in Redux), and optimize UI updates based on state changes.

```
// Redux example (simplified)
const store = createStore(reducer);

function increment() {
  store.dispatch({ type: "INCREMENT" });
}
```

3. Custom State Management: Tailored Solutions

If your application has unique requirements, you can create your own custom state management solution. This requires more effort but allows for maximum flexibility and control.

Choosing the Right Approach

The ideal state management approach depends on the size and complexity of your application, as well as your team's preferences and expertise. For small to medium-sized applications, local component state or a simple global store might be sufficient. Larger applications with complex state interactions often benefit from the structured approach of libraries like Redux or MobX.

Key Takeaways

State management is a critical aspect of building dynamic and complex JavaScript applications. It ensures data consistency, simplifies data sharing between components, and makes your application more predictable and maintainable. By understanding the different approaches to state management, you can choose the one that best suits your needs and build applications that are robust, scalable, and easy to manage.

State Management in Your Framework: Examples and Best Practices

Let's delve into practical examples of how you can implement state management within your JavaScript framework, showcasing both local component state and global state management approaches.

Local Component State: A Simple Counter

For simple components that don't need to share state with other parts of the application, local state management is often the most straightforward approach. Here's how you could implement a counter component with local state within your framework:

```
// Using class syntax for component definition
class CounterComponent {
  constructor() {
    this.state = { count: 0 };
  }

  increment() {
    this.setState({ count: this.state.count + 1 });
  }

  render() {
    return `
      <p>Count: ${this.state.count}</p>
      <button onclick="${this.increment.bind(this)}">Increment</button>
    `;
  }
}

// (Assume a function to attach the component to the DOM exists)
attachComponent(new CounterComponent(), document.body);
```

In this example:

1. The `CounterComponent` class maintains its state in the `this.state` object, which initially holds the `count` value.
2. The `increment` method updates the state by calling `this.setState`. This triggers a re-render of the component, updating the displayed count.

3. The `render` method generates the HTML for the component, including the current count and a button that, when clicked, calls `increment`.

Global State Management: A Centralized Store (Redux-like)

For larger applications, a global state management system like Redux provides a structured way to manage data shared across components.

```
// Simplified Redux-like implementation
const store = {
  state: { count: 0 },
  listeners: [],
  getState: () => store.state,
  subscribe: (listener) => store.listeners.push(listener),
  dispatch: (action) => {
    // ... (reducer logic to update state based on action) ...
    store.listeners.forEach(listener => listener()); // Notify components of
changes
  }
};

// Counter component (simplified)
function CounterComponent() {
  const state = store.getState();
  return `
    <p>Count: ${state.count}</p>
    <button onclick="store.dispatch({ type: 'INCREMENT' })">Increment</button>
  `;
}

store.subscribe(() => {
  // ... (update the UI when the store changes) ...
});
```

In this example:

1. The `store` object holds the global state and a list of subscribers.
2. Components subscribe to the store to be notified of changes.
3. Actions (e.g., `{ type: 'INCREMENT' }`) are dispatched to the store.
4. The reducer updates the state based on the action.
5. The store notifies subscribers, triggering UI updates.

Best Practices for State Management

- **Immutability:** Treat your state as immutable. When updating state, create a new copy rather than modifying the existing object directly. This helps with predictability and performance.
- **Predictable State Updates:** Use pure functions (reducers in Redux) to update your state. Pure functions take the current state and an action as input and return a new state without any side effects.
- **Centralized Store:** In global state management, use a single, centralized store to manage your entire application state. This makes it easier to reason about state changes and debug your application.
- **Clear Actions and Reducers:** In Redux-like systems, define clear actions that describe what happened (e.g., `INCREMENT`) and reducers that handle those actions and update the state accordingly.

By applying these best practices, you can build robust and scalable state management solutions within your custom JavaScript framework.

Chapter Summary

In this chapter, we explored advanced concepts that are essential for building robust and performant JavaScript frameworks. We delved into data binding, the mechanism that synchronizes your application's data with the user interface, creating a dynamic and interactive experience. We discussed different approaches to data binding, ranging from reactive event listeners to more sophisticated techniques like property descriptors and proxy objects.

We then introduced the virtual DOM (VDOM), a powerful technique for optimizing UI updates. We explained how the VDOM acts as an in-memory representation of the actual DOM, allowing for efficient diffing and minimal updates to the real DOM, resulting in significant performance improvements.

Finally, we tackled the complex topic of state management, emphasizing its crucial role in maintaining data consistency and ensuring smooth interactions between components in larger applications. We explored various state management approaches, from local component state to global state management libraries like Redux and MobX, as well as the possibility of creating custom solutions.

By understanding and applying these advanced framework concepts, you have gained the knowledge and tools to build more sophisticated and efficient JavaScript frameworks. With data binding, you can create dynamic and responsive UIs. With the virtual DOM, you can optimize performance and deliver smoother user experiences. And with robust state management, you can tame the complexity of large-scale applications, ensuring that your data is consistent and your components are synchronized.

In the next section of the book, we will explore advanced JavaScript techniques like asynchronous programming, functional programming, and object-oriented programming, further expanding your toolkit for building powerful and modern JavaScript applications.

Section V:
Advanced JavaScript Techniques

Asynchronous JavaScript: Callbacks, Promises, and Async/Await

Outline

- Understanding Asynchronous JavaScript
- Callbacks: The Foundation of Asynchronicity
- Promises: A Better Way to Handle Asynchronous Operations
- Async/Await: Making Asynchronous Code Look Synchronous
- Error Handling with Async/Await
- Chapter Summary

Understanding Asynchronous JavaScript

Asynchronous programming is a paradigm that allows your JavaScript code to perform tasks that take time (like network requests, user interactions, or timers) without blocking the main thread of execution. In simpler terms, it means your code can continue doing other things while it waits for those time-consuming tasks to complete.

Why Asynchronicity Matters

JavaScript, in its core, is single-threaded. This means it executes code line by line, one instruction at a time. However, certain operations can take a significant amount of time:

- **Network Requests:** Fetching data from a server or an API.
- **User Interactions:** Waiting for the user to click a button, fill out a form, or perform some other action.
- **Timers:** Executing code after a set delay (e.g., using `setTimeout`).

If JavaScript were to pause and wait for these operations to finish before moving on to the next line of code, your application would freeze, and the user experience would suffer. Imagine clicking a button and having the entire webpage freeze until the server responds! That's where asynchronous programming comes to the rescue.

The Non-Blocking Paradigm

Asynchronous code allows you to initiate a time-consuming operation and then continue executing other code while waiting for that operation to complete. When the operation finishes, JavaScript provides a way to notify you, often through a callback function or a Promise.

Real-World Examples

1. **Fetching Data from an API:** When you fetch data from a server, the request takes time to travel over the network and return with a response. Asynchronous code allows you to initiate the request, continue processing other tasks, and then handle the response when it arrives.
2. **Handling Button Clicks:** When a user clicks a button, you might want to perform some action in response, such as validating a form or sending data to the server. Asynchronous code ensures that the button click doesn't freeze the UI while your code is busy handling the request.
3. **Timers:** You can use `setTimeout` to schedule a function to run after a specified delay. This is essential for creating animations, visual effects, or simply delaying the execution of certain code blocks without blocking the rest of the script.

The Role of Callbacks, Promises, and Async/Await

JavaScript provides several mechanisms for handling asynchronous operations:

- **Callbacks:** The traditional way to handle asynchronicity, where you pass a function (the callback) to be executed when the operation completes.
- **Promises:** A more modern and structured way to represent the eventual result of an asynchronous operation.
- **Async/Await:** A syntactic sugar that makes asynchronous code look more like synchronous code, improving readability and maintainability.

In this chapter, we'll dive deeper into each of these mechanisms and learn how to use them effectively to write asynchronous JavaScript code that is responsive, efficient, and avoids the dreaded "callback hell."

Callbacks: The Foundation of Asynchronicity

Callbacks are the unsung heroes of asynchronous JavaScript. They are functions that you pass as arguments to other functions, with the expectation that the receiving function will call them back (execute them) at a later time when an asynchronous operation completes. In essence, callbacks provide a way for your code to say, "Hey, when you're done with that task, please let me know by calling this function."

How Callbacks Work

Let's illustrate the callback mechanism with a simple example using `setTimeout`:

```
function greet(name) {
  console.log(`Hello, ${name}!`);
}

setTimeout(greet, 2000, 'Alice'); // Call greet after 2 seconds
console.log("This message is executed first.");
```

Here's the breakdown:

1. `greet`: This is our callback function. It simply logs a greeting message to the console.
2. `setTimeout`: This built-in function takes three arguments:
    - The callback function (`greet`)
    - A delay in milliseconds (`2000`, meaning 2 seconds)
    - An argument to be passed to the callback function (`'Alice'`)
3. Asynchronous Execution: `setTimeout` schedules the `greet` function to be executed after 2 seconds, but it doesn't block the main thread. The code continues to execute, and "This message is executed first." is logged immediately.

4. Callback Execution: After 2 seconds, the timer expires, and the `setTimeout` function "calls back" the `greet` function, passing it the argument `'Alice'`. This results in "Hello, Alice!" being logged to the console.

Callbacks: The Foundation of Asynchronous JavaScript

Callbacks are deeply ingrained in JavaScript's asynchronous nature. They are used extensively in various scenarios:

- **Event Handling:** Event listeners (e.g., click, mouseover) are callback functions that are triggered when specific events occur.
- **AJAX Requests:** Functions like `fetch` or those from libraries like `axios` use callbacks to handle the results of network requests.
- **Node.js:** Callbacks are pervasive in Node.js for handling asynchronous file operations, network I/O, and other tasks.
- **Custom APIs and Libraries:** Many JavaScript libraries and frameworks rely on callbacks to provide flexibility and customization.

The Callback Challenge: Callback Hell

While callbacks are essential, their overuse can lead to code that's difficult to read and maintain. This is known as "callback hell" – nested callbacks within callbacks, creating a pyramid of doom.

```
asyncOperation1(function(result1) {
  asyncOperation2(result1, function(result2) {
    asyncOperation3(result2, function(result3) {
      // ... and so on
    });
  });
});
```

Fortunately, modern JavaScript offers solutions to this problem, such as Promises and async/await, which we'll explore shortly.

Callbacks in Practice: `setTimeout`, `setInterval`, and `fetch`

Let's see how callbacks work with some common JavaScript functions:

1. `setTimeout`: Executes a function once after a specified delay.

```
function sayHello(name) {
    console.log(`Hello, ${name}! (after 3 seconds)`);
}

setTimeout(sayHello, 3000, 'Alice');
// Output (after 3 seconds): "Hello, Alice! (after 3 seconds)"
```

2. `setInterval`: Repeatedly calls a function with a fixed time delay between each call.

```
function showTime() {
    console.log(`Current time: ${new Date().toLocaleTimeString()}`);
}

setInterval(showTime, 1000); // Call showTime every second
```

3. `fetch` (Web API): Retrieves data from a server.

```
fetch('https://jsonplaceholder.typicode.com/posts/1')
    .then(response => response.json())
    .then(data => console.log(data))
    .catch(error => console.error('Error:', error));
```

Here, the `.then()` methods take callback functions that are executed when the promise (representing the fetch operation) is resolved or rejected.

The Callback Hell Problem: Pyramids of Doom

While callbacks are essential, they can become messy when dealing with multiple asynchronous operations that depend on each other's results. This leads to deeply nested callbacks, creating code that's hard to read, understand, and debug.

```
doSomething(function(result1) {
    doSomethingElse(result1, function(result2) {
        doAnotherThing(result2, function(result3) {
            // ... more nested callbacks
        });
    });
});
```

This pyramid structure, known as "callback hell," makes code flow difficult to follow, increases the risk of errors, and hinders maintainability.

Mitigating Callback Hell: Enter Promises and Async/Await

To combat callback hell, modern JavaScript introduces Promises and async/await:

- **Promises:** Provide a more structured way to handle asynchronous operations, allowing you to chain them with `.then()` and `.catch()` for better error handling.
- **Async/Await:** Builds upon Promises and provides a cleaner syntax that makes asynchronous code look more like synchronous code.

In the following sections, we'll delve into these modern techniques, showing you how to escape the perils of callback hell and write more elegant and manageable asynchronous JavaScript code.

Promises: A Better Way to Handle Asynchronous Operations

Promises, introduced in ES6 (ECMAScript 2015), revolutionized how we handle asynchronous operations in JavaScript. They offer a more structured and intuitive approach compared to the traditional callback-based style, making asynchronous code more readable, maintainable, and less error-prone.

What is a Promise?

A Promise is an object that represents the eventual result of an asynchronous operation. It acts as a placeholder for a value that may not be available immediately. Promises can be in one of three states:

1. **Pending:** The initial state, indicating that the asynchronous operation is still in progress.
2. **Fulfilled (Resolved):** The operation has completed successfully, and the Promise now holds the resulting value.
3. **Rejected:** The operation has failed, and the Promise holds a reason (an error) for the failure.

Chaining Promises with `.then()`

One of the most powerful features of Promises is the ability to chain them together using the `.then()` method. This allows you to create a sequence of asynchronous operations that depend on each other.

```
fetch('https://api.example.com/data')
  .then(response => response.json())
  .then(data => console.log(data))
  .catch(error => console.error('Error:', error));
```

In this example, the first `.then()` block handles the response from the `fetch` request. It parses the JSON data and passes it to the next `.then()` block, which logs the data to the console. If any error occurs during the process, the `.catch()` block handles it.

Handling Success and Errors

- **`.then(onFulfilled, onRejected)`:** The `.then()` method takes two optional callback functions:
    - `onFulfilled`: Called when the Promise is fulfilled, receiving the result value as an argument.
    - `onRejected`: Called when the Promise is rejected, receiving the error reason as an argument.
- **`.catch(onRejected)`:** A shorthand for `.then(null, onRejected)`, used to handle errors that occur at any point in the Promise chain.

```
myPromise
  .then(result => {
    // Handle success here
    console.log(result);
  })
  .catch(error => {
    // Handle errors here
    console.error(error);
  });
```

Promises vs. Callbacks: A Clear Advantage

Promises offer several advantages over traditional callbacks:

- **Improved Readability:** Promise chains are more linear and easier to follow than nested callbacks.
- **Better Error Handling:** The `.catch()` method simplifies error handling and ensures that errors are caught throughout the chain.
- **Avoiding Callback Hell:** Promises help avoid the deeply nested callback structures that can make code difficult to maintain.
- **Cleaner Code:** The Promise syntax is generally more concise and expressive than callbacks.

By embracing Promises, you can write cleaner, more reliable, and more enjoyable asynchronous JavaScript code. They are the foundation for more advanced asynchronous patterns like async/await, which we'll explore in the next section.

Promises in Practice: Fetching Data and Beyond

Let's solidify our understanding of Promises with practical examples using the `fetch` API and other asynchronous functions.

Example 1: Fetching Data from an API

```
fetch('https://api.example.com/data')
  .then(response => {
    if (!response.ok) {
      throw new Error(`HTTP error! status: ${response.status}`);
    }
    return response.json();
  })
  .then(data => {
    // Process the fetched data here
    console.log(data);
  })
  .catch(error => {
    console.error('Error fetching data:', error);
  });
```

In this example:

1. We use the `fetch` function to request data from an API. This returns a Promise that resolves with a `Response` object.
2. The first `.then()` block checks if the response is successful (status code 200-299). If not, it throws an error. Otherwise, it parses the response as JSON and returns another Promise.
3. The second `.then()` block receives the parsed JSON data and logs it to the console.
4. If any error occurs during the fetch process, the `.catch()` block is executed, logging the error message.

Example 2: Custom Promise with `setTimeout`

```
function delay(ms) {
  return new Promise(resolve => setTimeout(resolve, ms));
}

delay(2000)
  .then(() => console.log('Delayed message after 2 seconds'))
  .catch(error => console.error('Error:', error));
```

Here, we create a custom `delay` function that returns a Promise. The Promise is resolved after the specified delay (2000 milliseconds). We then use `.then()` to log a message when the Promise is fulfilled.

Example 3: Chaining Promises

```
function getUser(userId) {
  return fetch(`https://api.example.com/users/${userId}`)
    .then(response => response.json());
}

function getPosts(userId) {
  return fetch(`https://api.example.com/posts?userId=${userId}`)
    .then(response => response.json());
}

getUser(1)
  .then(user => {
    console.log('User:', user);
    return getPosts(user.id);
  })
```

```
  .then(posts => console.log('Posts:', posts))
  .catch(error => console.error('Error:', error));
```

This example demonstrates how you can chain Promises to perform dependent asynchronous operations. First, we fetch user data, then we fetch posts for that user, handling errors gracefully at each step.

Key Points

- Promises provide a cleaner and more structured way to handle asynchronous operations than callbacks.
- You can chain Promises using `.then()` to create sequences of dependent operations.
- The `.catch()` method simplifies error handling for both synchronous and asynchronous errors in a Promise chain.

Promises are a powerful tool in your JavaScript arsenal. By mastering them, you can write asynchronous code that is more readable, maintainable, and less prone to errors.

Async/Await: Making Asynchronous Code Look Synchronous

While Promises offer a significant improvement over callbacks, they can still be a bit cumbersome to work with, especially when dealing with multiple asynchronous operations. Async/await, introduced in ES2017 (ES8), builds upon Promises and provides a cleaner and more intuitive syntax for writing asynchronous code.

What is Async/Await?

- **async:** A keyword used to declare a function as asynchronous. An async function always returns a Promise, even if you don't explicitly return one.
- **`await`:** A keyword used inside an `async` function to pause the execution of the function until a Promise resolves. The resolved value of the Promise is then returned.

The Magic of Async/Await: Synchronous-Like Code

With async/await, you can write asynchronous code that looks and feels almost like synchronous code. Let's see an example:

```
async function fetchData() {
  try {
    const response = await fetch('https://api.example.com/data');
    const data = await response.json();
    console.log(data);
  } catch (error) {
    console.error('Error fetching data:', error);
  }
}

fetchData();
```

This code looks remarkably similar to synchronous code. You call `fetchData()`, and it seems like the code waits for the `fetch` operation to complete before moving on to parse the JSON data. However, under the hood, `await` pauses the execution of `fetchData()` until the Promise returned by `fetch` resolves.

How It Works Under the Hood

The `await` keyword essentially "unwraps" the Promise, giving you direct access to the resolved value. It also elegantly handles errors using `try...catch` blocks, making error management much more straightforward.

Benefits of Async/Await

- **Readability:** Async/await code is cleaner, more concise, and easier to follow than Promise chains.
- **Error Handling:** `try...catch` blocks provide a familiar way to handle errors in asynchronous code.
- **Debugging:** Async/await makes it easier to debug asynchronous code because you can step through it line by line, just like synchronous code.
- **Maintainability:** Asynchronous code written with async/await is easier to maintain and refactor.

Important Notes

- **`async` Functions Always Return Promises:** Even if your `async` function doesn't explicitly return a value, it will implicitly return a Promise that resolves with `undefined`.
- **`await` Only Works Inside `async` Functions:** You can only use the `await` keyword within functions declared with the `async` keyword.

Async/await is a game-changer for writing asynchronous JavaScript code. It provides a more intuitive and elegant syntax, making asynchronous operations feel more like synchronous ones. By mastering this technique, you'll be able to write cleaner, more maintainable, and less error-prone asynchronous code.

Async/Await in Action: Taming Asynchronous Chaos

Let's explore how async/await can be used to write cleaner and more manageable asynchronous code, especially in scenarios where you have multiple dependent operations.

Example 1: Fetching and Processing Multiple Resources

```
async function fetchAndProcessData() {
  try {
    const userResponse = await fetch('https://api.example.com/user/1');
    const userData = await userResponse.json();

    const postsResponse = await
fetch(`https://api.example.com/posts?userId=${userData.id}`);
    const postsData = await postsResponse.json();

    console.log("User:", userData);
    console.log("Posts:", postsData);
  } catch (error) {
    console.error("Error fetching data:", error);
  }
}

fetchAndProcessData();
```

In this example, we first fetch user data, then use the `userId` from the response to fetch that user's posts. The `await` keyword pauses execution at each step until the Promise resolves, making the code flow linearly and easy to follow.

Example 2: Handling Multiple API Calls Concurrently

```
async function fetchMultipleResources() {
  try {
    const [userResponse, postsResponse] = await Promise.all([
      fetch('https://api.example.com/user/1'),
      fetch('https://api.example.com/posts')
    ]);

    const userData = await userResponse.json();
    const postsData = await postsResponse.json();

    console.log("User:", userData);
    console.log("Posts:", postsData);
  } catch (error) {
    console.error("Error fetching data:", error);
  }
}

fetchMultipleResources();
```

Here, we use `Promise.all` to fetch user data and posts concurrently. The `await` keyword waits for both Promises to resolve before proceeding, ensuring that both `userData` and `postsData` are available.

Example 3: Error Handling with Async/Await

```
async function fetchData(url) {
  try {
    const response = await fetch(url);
    if (!response.ok) {
      throw new Error(`HTTP error! status: ${response.status}`);
    }
    return await response.json();
  } catch (error) {
    console.error("Error fetching data:", error);
    throw error; // Re-throw the error to be handled by the caller if needed
  }
}
```

In this example, the `fetchData` function uses a `try...catch` block to handle errors that might occur during the fetch operation. If an error occurs, it's logged to the console and re-thrown to allow the caller of the function to handle it as well.

Benefits of Async/Await

- **Readability:** The code reads like synchronous code, making it much easier to understand and reason about.
- **Maintainability:** Error handling and control flow are more intuitive and easier to manage.
- **Debugging:** You can use standard debugging tools to step through `async` functions line by line, just like synchronous code.

By embracing async/await, you can transform your asynchronous code from a tangled mess of callbacks into a well-structured, maintainable, and elegant piece of software.

Error Handling with Async/Await

One of the most significant advantages of async/await is the streamlined approach to error handling it provides. By using familiar `try...catch` blocks, you can easily catch errors that occur during asynchronous operations, making your code more robust and easier to debug.

The `try...catch` Block: Your Safety Net

When dealing with asynchronous code, errors can pop up in unexpected places. With async/await, you can wrap your asynchronous operations within a `try...catch` block. If an error occurs during the execution of the `try` block, control immediately jumps to the `catch` block, allowing you to gracefully handle the error.

Example: Error Handling in `fetch`

```
async function fetchData(url) {
  try {
    const response = await fetch(url);
    if (!response.ok) { // Check for HTTP errors
      throw new Error(`HTTP error! status: ${response.status}`);
    }
    const data = await response.json();
    return data;
  } catch (error) {
    console.error("Error fetching data:", error);
    // Handle the error appropriately (e.g., display an error message to the
user)
    return null; // Or return a default value
  }
}

fetchData('https://api.example.com/data')
  .then(data => {
    if (data) {
      // Process the data
    } else {
      // Handle the case where fetchData returned null due to an error
    }
  });
```

Here's the breakdown:

1. `try`: The code within the `try` block contains the asynchronous operations (fetching data and parsing JSON).
2. `await`: The `await` keyword pauses the execution of the function until the Promise returned by `fetch` is settled (either fulfilled or rejected).
3. Error Checking: We check if the `response.ok` property is `true`. If not, it indicates an HTTP error, and we explicitly throw an `Error`.
4. `catch`: If an error occurs (either during the fetch, the response check, or the JSON parsing), the `catch` block is executed. We log the error to the console and optionally return a default value or throw the error again for the caller to handle.
5. Error Propagation: If the `fetchData` function returns null due to an error, the `.then()` block of the caller can handle this specific case.

Advantages of Error Handling with Async/Await

- **Clarity:** The error handling logic is located right next to the asynchronous operation, making the code easier to follow.
- **Flexibility:** You can decide how to handle errors in each `catch` block, tailoring the response to the specific situation.
- **Centralized Error Handling:** You can consolidate error handling logic in a single place, improving code maintainability.
- **Improved Debugging:** Debugging is simpler because you can step through the `async` function line by line, even when errors occur.

Best Practices for Error Handling

- **Always Use `try...catch`:** Wrap your `await` statements within `try...catch` blocks to catch any potential errors.
- **Handle Errors Gracefully:** Log error messages to the console for debugging and provide user-friendly feedback in the UI.
- **Consider Re-throwing Errors:** In some cases, you might want to re-throw the error in the `catch` block to allow higher-level components or error handling mechanisms to deal with it.
- **Don't Overuse `catch`:** Avoid nesting too many `try...catch` blocks, as this can make your code less readable.
- **Use Promise Rejection:** If you're creating your own Promises, be sure to use `Promise.reject()` to signal errors.

By following these best practices and leveraging the power of async/await and `try...catch`, you can write asynchronous JavaScript code that is not only more readable but also more robust and resilient to errors.

Chapter Summary

In this chapter, we delved into the asynchronous nature of JavaScript, where certain operations like network requests, user interactions, and timers occur outside the main flow of code execution. We explored three key mechanisms for managing asynchronicity:

1. **Callbacks:** The traditional and fundamental way to handle asynchronous operations by passing functions to be executed upon completion. We saw how callbacks are used in functions like `setTimeout`, `setInterval`, and `fetch`, but also discussed the challenge of "callback hell" when dealing with multiple nested callbacks.
2. **Promises:** A more modern and structured approach to asynchronicity that represents the eventual result of an operation. We explored the three states of a Promise (pending, fulfilled, rejected) and how to chain them using `.then()` and `.catch()` for better error handling. We also demonstrated the use of Promises with the `fetch` API and other asynchronous functions.
3. **Async/Await:** A powerful syntactic sugar that simplifies asynchronous code and makes it look more like synchronous code. We learned how to use the `async` and `await` keywords to pause execution until a Promise resolves and how to handle errors gracefully with `try...catch` blocks. We saw how async/await improves code readability, maintainability, and error handling compared to callbacks and Promise chains.

By mastering these asynchronous techniques, you are equipped to write more responsive, efficient, and reliable JavaScript code that can handle real-world scenarios like network requests, user interactions, and background tasks without blocking the main thread. This knowledge will be invaluable as you tackle more advanced JavaScript projects and dive deeper into the realm of asynchronous programming.

Functional Programming in JavaScript: Pure Functions, Immutability, Currying

Outline

- Embracing a Functional Mindset
- Pure Functions: Predictable and Reliable
- Immutability: Avoiding Unwanted Changes
- Currying: Transforming Functions
- Composing Functions: Building Blocks for Flexibility
- Practical Benefits of Functional Programming in JavaScript
- Chapter Summary

Embracing a Functional Mindset

Functional programming (FP) is a programming paradigm that offers a different way of thinking about how to structure and solve problems in your code. It shifts the focus from *how* things are done (imperative) to *what* is being done (declarative), emphasizing a few core principles:

Pure Functions: The cornerstone of FP. These are functions that:

- Always produce the same output for the same input.
- Have no side effects, meaning they don't modify external state or interact with the outside world in any way.

Immutability: Data is treated as immutable, meaning it cannot be changed once created. Instead of modifying existing values, you create new ones with the desired changes.

Avoiding Side Effects: Side effects are any actions a function performs besides returning a value. This includes modifying variables outside its scope, performing I/O operations, or changing the state of the program in any way. FP advocates for minimizing side effects.

First-Class Functions: Functions are treated as values. You can pass them as arguments, return them from other functions, and store them in variables, just like you would with numbers or strings.

How FP Differs from Imperative Programming

Feature	Imperative Programming	Functional Programming
Emphasis	How to do things (statements, loops)	What to do (expressions, functions)
State	Mutable	Immutable (preferably)
Side Effects	Common	Minimized or isolated
Functions	Often second-class citizens	First-class values
Composition	Less common	Encouraged (higher-order functions)

Benefits of Functional Programming

Adopting a functional programming mindset in JavaScript can lead to:

- **Improved Readability:** Code is more declarative and concise, focusing on what to do rather than how to do it.
- **Increased Maintainability:** Smaller, pure functions are easier to understand, test, and modify independently.
- **Reduced Bugs:** The absence of side effects makes code more predictable and less prone to unexpected errors.
- **Better Testability:** Pure functions are easier to test in isolation since they have no dependencies on external state.
- **Concurrency-Friendly:** Immutability simplifies concurrent programming by avoiding race conditions and shared state issues.

Example: Imperative vs. Functional

```
// Imperative
let numbers = [1, 2, 3, 4];
let doubled = [];
for (let i = 0; i < numbers.length; i++) {
  doubled.push(numbers[i] * 2);
}

// Functional
const numbers = [1, 2, 3, 4];
const doubled = numbers.map(x => x * 2);
```

The functional version is more concise and clearly expresses the intention of doubling each element.

Embracing the Mindset

Functional programming is not an all-or-nothing approach. You can gradually incorporate its principles into your JavaScript code to reap the benefits. Even small steps, like using more pure functions and immutable data structures, can lead to significant improvements in code quality and maintainability.

Pure Functions: Predictable and Reliable

In the realm of functional programming, pure functions are like the bedrock of reliability. They are the building blocks upon which you can construct solid, predictable, and easily testable code.

What Defines a Pure Function?

A pure function adheres to two fundamental rules:

1. **Deterministic Output:** Given the same input, a pure function always produces the same output. There's no randomness or hidden state involved.
2. **No Side Effects:** A pure function doesn't modify any external state, such as global variables, or perform any actions that interact with the outside world (like network requests or console logging). Its only job is to compute and return a value.

Pure vs. Impure: A Contrast

```
// Pure Function
function add(x, y) {
  return x + y;
}
```

```
// Impure Function
let total = 0;
function addToTotal(value) {
  total += value; // Modifies external variable 'total'
  console.log(total); // Side effect: logging to the console
}
```

In this example, `add` is pure. It consistently returns the sum of its arguments without any side effects. In contrast, `addToTotal` is impure. It modifies the external variable `total` and logs to the console, both of which are observable side effects.

Why Pure Functions Matter

Pure functions bring a host of benefits to your code:

- **Predictability:** You can always rely on a pure function to give you the same result for the same input, making your code easier to reason about.
- **Testability:** Pure functions are a dream to test. You provide the input, and you know exactly what output to expect.
- **Composability:** You can easily chain pure functions together to create more complex behaviors. The output of one function becomes the input of another, like building blocks.
- **Parallelism:** Pure functions are inherently safe for parallel execution because they don't depend on or modify shared state.

Reasoning with Pure Functions: An Example

Let's say you have a function `calculatePrice(item, quantity)` that calculates the total price of a set of items. If it's a pure function, you can confidently call it multiple times with the same arguments and know that the result will always be the same. This makes it easier to debug and reason about your code, as you can isolate the function and verify its behavior without worrying about external influences.

Embracing Pure Functions

While not every function can or should be pure (e.g., functions that interact with the user or fetch data), striving for pure functions wherever possible can significantly improve the quality of your JavaScript code. By keeping your functions self-contained and focused on their core responsibility, you'll create code that is more reliable, testable, and easier to understand.

Immutability: Avoiding Unwanted Changes

Immutability, in the context of functional programming and JavaScript, means treating data as unchangeable. Once you create an object or array, its state remains fixed. You can't modify it directly; instead, you create new objects or arrays with the desired modifications.

Why Immutability Matters

Immutability offers several compelling benefits:

1. **Predictability:** Immutable data structures behave consistently throughout your program. You never have to worry about a function unexpectedly modifying your data, leading to hidden bugs.
2. **Easier Debugging:** Tracking changes in immutable data is straightforward. You can compare the old and new versions of an object or array to pinpoint exactly what changed.
3. **Simplified State Management:** In applications with complex state, immutability simplifies reasoning about how state changes over time. It makes it easier to track state transitions and understand how different parts of your application interact with the state.

4. **Concurrency Safety:** Immutable data is inherently safe for concurrent operations. Multiple parts of your code can access and use the same immutable data without the risk of race conditions or data corruption.

Working with Immutability in JavaScript

JavaScript doesn't enforce immutability by default, but you can adopt practices and tools to make your data immutable:

1. **The Spread Operator (`...`) and `Object.assign()`:**

```
const originalArray = [1, 2, 3];
const newArray = [...originalArray, 4]; // Add an element without
modifying originalArray
console.log(originalArray); // [1, 2, 3]

const originalObject = { name: "Alice", age: 30 };
const updatedObject = { ...originalObject, age: 31 };
console.log(originalObject); // { name: "Alice", age: 30 }
```

2. **Array Methods that Return New Arrays:**

   Methods like `map`, `filter`, `concat`, and `slice` return new arrays instead of modifying the original array.

```
const numbers = [1, 2, 3];
const doubled = numbers.map(x => x * 2); // [2, 4, 6]
```

3. **Immutable.js Library:**

   For more complex scenarios, you can use the Immutable.js library, which provides a rich set of immutable data structures and functions for working with them efficiently.

```
const { Map } = require('immutable');
const map1 = Map({ a: 1, b: 2, c: 3 });
const map2 = map1.set('b', 50); // Returns a new map with the update
console.log(map1.get('b')); // 2
console.log(map2.get('b')); // 50
```

A Note of Caution

Immutability can sometimes lead to increased memory usage because you're creating new objects or arrays instead of modifying existing ones. However, in most cases, the benefits of immutability outweigh this minor drawback.

By embracing immutability in your JavaScript code, you'll be taking a significant step towards writing cleaner, more reliable, and easier-to-reason-about code.

Currying: Transforming Functions

Currying is a functional programming technique that involves transforming a function that takes multiple arguments into a sequence of nested functions, each taking a single argument. It's like slicing a pizza into individual slices instead of eating it whole.

How Currying Works

Consider a function `add(x, y)` that adds two numbers. A curried version of this function would look like this:

```
function add(x) {
  return function(y) {
    return x + y;
  };
}

const add5 = add(5); // Returns a new function that adds 5 to its argument
console.log(add5(3)); // Output: 8
```

In this example:

1. `add(x)` is called with the argument 5.
2. It returns a new function `(y) => x + y` with x (the value 5) captured in its closure.
3. We assign this new function to `add5`.
4. When we call `add5(3)`, it effectively executes `5 + 3` and returns 8.

Currying vs. Partial Application

Currying and partial application are related but distinct concepts:

- **Currying:** Always transforms a multi-argument function into a chain of single-argument functions.
- **Partial Application:** Can fix some arguments of a function, but doesn't necessarily create a chain of single-argument functions.

  ```
  // Partial Application
  const add10 = add.bind(null, 10); // Fixes the first argument as 10
  console.log(add10(7)); // Output: 17

  // Currying
  const addCurried = x => y => x + y;
  const add3 = addCurried(3);
  console.log(add3(4)); // Output: 7
  ```

Benefits of Currying

- **Flexibility:** You can create specialized functions by partially applying arguments.
- **Composability:** Curried functions are easier to compose using higher-order functions.
- **Readability:** The code can be more concise and easier to understand in some cases.

Practical Examples

1. **Logging with Context:**

   ```
   function log(level, message) {
     console.log(`[${level}]: ${message}`);
   }

   const logError = log.bind(null, "ERROR"); // Partial application
   logError("Something went wrong!");
   ```

2. **Function Composition:**

   ```
   const compose = (f, g) => x => f(g(x));
   ```

```
const double = x => x * 2;
const square = x => x * x;

const doubleAndSquare = compose(square, double);
console.log(doubleAndSquare(3)); // Output: 36 (double(3) = 6, square(6)
= 36)
```

By understanding currying, you can write more flexible and composable JavaScript code. It's a technique that can be applied in various scenarios to create specialized functions and improve the structure of your code.

Composing Functions: Building Blocks for Flexibility

Function composition is a powerful technique in functional programming that allows you to create complex functions by combining simpler functions. It's like building with Lego blocks – you take smaller, reusable functions and snap them together to create a larger structure.

The Essence of Function Composition

The core idea of function composition is to take the output of one function and use it as the input to another function. This creates a chain of functions where the result of each function flows into the next.

Benefits of Function Composition

1. **Modularity:** Break down complex logic into smaller, manageable functions that are easier to understand, test, and maintain.
2. **Reusability:** Each function in the composition can be reused independently in other parts of your code.
3. **Readability:** Function composition expresses the flow of data clearly, making your code more declarative and self-documenting.
4. **Testability:** Smaller, independent functions are easier to test in isolation.

Composing with Higher-Order Functions

JavaScript's built-in higher-order functions like `map`, `filter`, and `reduce` are excellent tools for function composition.

```
const numbers = [1, 2, 3, 4];

const doubledAndFiltered = numbers
  .map(x => x * 2)          // [2, 4, 6, 8]
  .filter(x => x > 5);      // [6, 8]

const sumOfDoubledAndFiltered = doubledAndFiltered.reduce((acc, x) => acc + x,
0); // 14
```

In this example, we compose three functions: `map` to double each number, `filter` to keep only numbers greater than 5, and `reduce` to calculate the sum.

The Pipe Operator (Optional)

In modern JavaScript, you can use the pipe operator (`|>`) to make function composition more visually appealing:

```
const result = numbers
```

```
  |> double
  |> filter(x => x > 5)
  |> reduce((acc, x) => acc + x, 0);
```

This reads as "numbers, then double, then filter, then reduce." (Note: Pipe operator support depends on your JavaScript environment. It's available in Node.js 16+ and some browsers.)

Composing with Libraries: Ramda (Example)

Libraries like Ramda provide utilities like `compose` and `pipe` to make function composition even easier and more powerful.

```
const R = require('ramda');

const double = x => x * 2;
const addOne = x => x + 1;
const square = x => x * x;

const transform = R.pipe(double, addOne, square); // Composition with pipe
console.log(transform(3)); // Output: 49
```

Key Takeaway

Function composition is a key technique in functional programming that allows you to build complex logic from simpler, reusable functions. By embracing this approach, you can create more modular, maintainable, and expressive code. Whether you use higher-order functions, the pipe operator, or dedicated libraries like Ramda, function composition empowers you to write cleaner and more elegant JavaScript.

Practical Benefits of Functional Programming in JavaScript

Adopting functional programming (FP) principles in JavaScript offers a multitude of benefits that can transform how you approach development, leading to more reliable, maintainable, and elegant code. Let's delve into the practical advantages of FP and see how it shines in real-world scenarios.

1. Readability: Code That Speaks Volumes

FP's emphasis on pure functions and immutability results in code that's easier to read and understand. Pure functions, with their predictable behavior and lack of side effects, act like self-contained black boxes. You can focus on their input and output without worrying about hidden dependencies or unexpected modifications.

```
// Pure function:
const square = x => x * x; // Clear, concise, and predictable

// Impure function:
let result = 0;
function squareAndStore(x) {
  result = x * x;  // Modifies external state
  return result;
}
```

The pure `square` function is immediately understandable, while the impure `squareAndStore` function introduces hidden complexity due to its side effect.

2. Maintainability: Building Blocks of Resilience

By breaking down your code into small, reusable, and pure functions, you create building blocks that are easy to test, refactor, and combine. Changes in one function are less likely to affect others, making your codebase more robust and adaptable to future requirements.

3. Testability: Testing Made Easy

Pure functions are a tester's dream. With no external dependencies, testing them involves simply providing input and verifying the output. This leads to more reliable tests and greater confidence in the correctness of your code.

```
// Testing the 'square' function
const assert = require('assert');
assert.strictEqual(square(4), 16); // This test will pass reliably
```

4. Concurrency: Smooth Sailing in Parallel Waters

Immutable data structures are a natural fit for concurrent programming. Since they cannot be changed, multiple threads or processes can safely access the same data without the risk of race conditions or data corruption.

```
const originalList = [1, 2, 3];
const newList = originalList.concat([4]); // Create a new list without
modifying the original
```

5. Debugging: Tracing the Path of Data

The absence of side effects in functional code makes it significantly easier to track the flow of data and pinpoint the source of errors. You can focus on the input and output of functions without worrying about hidden modifications happening elsewhere.

Real-World Applications

- **Data Transformation:** Libraries like Ramda provide a wealth of higher-order functions for transforming and manipulating data in a functional style.
- **State Management:** Libraries like Redux embrace immutability and pure functions to manage application state predictably.
- **React Components:** React's functional components encourage a functional approach by treating components as pure functions of their props.

By adopting functional programming principles, you can elevate your JavaScript code to a new level of clarity, reliability, and maintainability. While JavaScript isn't a purely functional language, embracing the functional mindset can empower you to write code that is more elegant, robust, and easier to reason about.

Chapter Summary

In this chapter, we explored the principles and practices of functional programming (FP) in JavaScript. We learned how to shift our mindset from imperative thinking (how to do things) to declarative thinking (what to do), emphasizing the use of pure functions and immutable data.

Pure functions, the cornerstone of FP, offer predictability and testability by ensuring that the same input always produces the same output without side effects. Immutability, the practice of not changing data once created, further enhances code reliability and simplifies state management.

We also delved into currying, a technique for transforming multi-argument functions into a chain of single-argument functions, promoting flexibility and composability. Finally, we explored function composition, the art of combining simple functions to create more complex ones, fostering modularity and code reuse.

By adopting functional programming principles, even gradually, you can write JavaScript code that is more readable, maintainable, testable, and robust. These principles empower you to tackle complexity with greater confidence and clarity, leading to more enjoyable and productive development experiences.

Object-Oriented Programming (OOP) in JavaScript: Classes, Inheritance, and Polymorphism

Outline

- OOP Concepts in JavaScript
- Classes: A Blueprint for Objects
- Inheritance: Extending Functionality
- Polymorphism: Many Forms, One Interface
- Chapter Summary

OOP Concepts in JavaScript

While JavaScript is not traditionally a class-based language like Java or C++, it has embraced many core principles of Object-Oriented Programming (OOP). Let's explore these concepts and how they manifest in the world of JavaScript.

The Four Pillars of OOP

1. **Encapsulation:** Think of encapsulation as creating a protective capsule around your data and the functions that operate on it. In JavaScript, objects serve as these capsules. You bundle related data (properties) and behavior (methods) together within an object, creating a self-contained unit.
2. **Abstraction:** Abstraction means simplifying complex systems by hiding unnecessary details and exposing only essential features. In JavaScript, you achieve abstraction by creating well-defined interfaces for your objects. This allows other parts of your code to interact with the object without needing to know its internal implementation details.
3. **Inheritance:** Inheritance is the process of creating new objects (child objects) based on existing objects (parent objects). The child objects inherit properties and behaviors from their parents, allowing you to reuse code and create hierarchical relationships between objects.
4. **Polymorphism:** This concept refers to the ability of objects of different types to be treated interchangeably through a common interface. In JavaScript, polymorphism is achieved by having objects of different classes implement the same methods, but with their own specific implementations.

JavaScript's Prototypal Inheritance Model

Unlike class-based languages, where objects are created from class blueprints, JavaScript uses a prototype-based inheritance model. Every object in JavaScript has a special property called `[[Prototype]]` (or `__proto__`) that links it to another object, its prototype. This creates a prototype chain, where objects inherit properties and methods from their prototypes, forming a hierarchical structure.

The Rise of Classes (ES6+)

While JavaScript's prototypal inheritance is powerful, it can be less intuitive for developers coming from class-based languages. To address this, ES6 introduced a class syntax that acts as a more familiar way to define and work with objects.

```
class Animal {
  constructor(name) {
    this.name = name;
  }
```

```
  makeSound() {
    console.log("Generic animal sound!");
  }
}

class Dog extends Animal {
  constructor(name, breed) {
    super(name);
    this.breed = breed;
  }

  makeSound() {
    console.log("Woof!");
  }
}
```

In this example, the Dog class inherits from the `Animal` class using the `extends` keyword. It overrides the `makeSound` method to provide its own specific implementation.

Key Takeaway

While JavaScript's object model is based on prototypes, not classes, it still embraces the fundamental concepts of OOP: encapsulation, abstraction, inheritance, and polymorphism. ES6 classes provide a convenient syntax for working with objects and inheritance, making JavaScript more approachable for developers from diverse backgrounds. As you delve deeper into OOP in JavaScript, you'll discover how to leverage these concepts to build more structured, modular, and maintainable code.

Classes: A Blueprint for Objects

In the ever-evolving landscape of JavaScript, the introduction of classes in ES6 (ECMAScript 2015) marked a significant step towards embracing object-oriented principles. Classes provide a more structured and familiar way to define blueprints for creating objects, making your code more organized and easier to reason about.

The Class Keyword: A New Syntax, a Familiar Concept

At its core, a JavaScript class is a template for creating objects. It's like a blueprint that defines the properties (data) and methods (functions) that objects created from this class will have. You declare a class using the `class` keyword, followed by the class name and a pair of curly braces:

```
class Car {
  // Class body (properties and methods go here)
}
```

Constructors: Building the Foundation

Within a class, the `constructor` method is a special function that is called when you create a new instance of the class (using the `new` keyword). The constructor's primary responsibility is to initialize the object's properties.

```
class Car {
  constructor(brand, model, year) {
    this.brand = brand;
```

```
    this.model = model;
    this.year = year;
  }
}
```

In this example, the `Car` class has a constructor that takes three arguments: `brand`, `model`, and `year`. It uses the `this` keyword to assign these values to the corresponding properties of the new `Car` object.

Methods: Defining Behavior

Methods are functions defined within a class. They provide the actions or behaviors that objects of the class can perform.

```
class Car {
  // ... (constructor) ...

  startEngine() {
    console.log("Vroom! Engine started.");
  }
}
```

In this case, the `Car` class has a `startEngine` method that logs a message to the console when called.

Class Properties (ES6+): A Modern Touch

While not strictly related to OOP principles, ES6 introduced a feature called class properties, allowing you to declare properties directly within the class definition.

```
class Car {
  numberOfWheels = 4; // Class property

  constructor(brand, model, year) {
    // ...
  }
}
```

Static Methods: Belonging to the Class

Static methods are methods that belong to the class itself, not to instances of the class. They are typically used for utility functions or operations that don't depend on the state of a specific object.

```
class MathUtils {
  static add(x, y) {
    return x + y;
  }
}

console.log(MathUtils.add(5, 3)); // Output: 8
```

In this example, `MathUtils.add()` is a static method that can be called directly on the `MathUtils` class.

By understanding the syntax and features of classes, you can leverage the power of OOP in JavaScript to create well-structured, maintainable, and reusable code.

Code Examples of Defining Classes with Constructors, Methods, and Class Properties

Let's illustrate how to define classes in JavaScript with constructors, methods, and class properties, along with code examples:

Basic Class with Constructor:

```
class Person {
  constructor(name, age) {
    this.name = name;
    this.age = age;
  }
}

const alice = new Person("Alice", 30);
console.log(alice.name); // Output: "Alice"
console.log(alice.age);  // Output: 30
```

In this basic example, the `Person` class has a `constructor` that initializes the name and age properties. We create an instance (`alice`) using the new keyword.

Class with Methods:

```
class Rectangle {
  constructor(width, height) {
    this.width = width;
    this.height = height;
  }

  calculateArea() {
    return this.width * this.height;
  }
}

const myRectangle = new Rectangle(5, 10);
console.log(myRectangle.calculateArea()); // Output: 50
```

Here, the `Rectangle` class has a `calculateArea` method that performs a calculation based on the object's properties.

Class with Properties (ES6+):

```
class Circle {
  PI = 3.14159; // Class property

  constructor(radius) {
    this.radius = radius;
  }

  calculateArea() {
    return this.PI * this.radius * this.radius;
  }
}

const myCircle = new Circle(5);
console.log(myCircle.calculateArea()); // Output: 78.53975
```

The `Circle` class has a `PI` property directly defined within the class body (this syntax is supported in ES6 and later).

Class with Static Method:

```
class StringUtils {
  static reverseString(str) {
    return str.split('').reverse().join('');
  }
}

console.log(StringUtils.reverseString("hello")); // Output: "olleh"
```

The `StringUtils` class has a static method `reverseString` that can be called directly on the class, without needing to create an object instance.

Putting It All Together:

```
class Book {
  genre = "Fiction"; // Class property

  constructor(title, author, pages) {
    this.title = title;
    this.author = author;
    this.pages = pages;
  }

  getDescription() {
    return `${this.title} by ${this.author} (${this.pages} pages)`;
  }

  static compareByPages(book1, book2) {
    return book1.pages - book2.pages;
  }
}
```

In this comprehensive example, the Book class has a constructor, methods, a class property, and a static method, showcasing various aspects of class definitions in JavaScript.

Inheritance: Extending Functionality

Inheritance is a cornerstone of object-oriented programming (OOP) that allows you to create new classes (child classes or derived classes) based on existing classes (parent classes or base classes). This concept promotes code reusability and establishes hierarchical relationships between classes, making your code more organized and maintainable.

The `extends` Keyword: Establishing the Relationship

The `extends` keyword is the key to creating inheritance relationships in JavaScript classes. It links a child class to its parent class, enabling the child to inherit the parent's properties and methods.

```
class Animal { // Parent Class
  constructor(name) {
    this.name = name;
  }
```

```
  makeSound() {
    console.log("Generic animal sound!");
  }
}

class Dog extends Animal { // Child Class (inherits from Animal)
  constructor(name, breed) {
    super(name); // Call the parent's constructor
    this.breed = breed;
  }

  makeSound() {
    console.log("Woof!"); // Overriding the parent's makeSound method
  }
}

const myDog = new Dog("Buddy", "Golden Retriever");
myDog.makeSound(); // Output: "Woof!" (calls the overridden method)
```

In this example, the Dog class inherits from the `Animal` class using the `extends` keyword. This means that Dog automatically has access to the properties and methods defined in `Animal`.

The `super` Keyword: Connecting to the Parent

The `super` keyword plays a crucial role in inheritance. It has two main purposes:

1. **Calling Parent Constructor:** Inside a child class constructor, you must call `super()` before using `this`. This ensures that the parent class constructor is executed, initializing the inherited properties.
2. **Accessing Parent Methods:** Within a child class method, you can use `super.method_name()` to access and call methods defined on the parent class.

Method Overriding: Customization for the Child

Inheritance doesn't mean blind replication. A child class can override methods inherited from its parent class. This allows you to customize the behavior of the child object while still retaining the overall structure and functionality of the parent class.

In our example, the Dog class overrides the `makeSound` method to produce a more specific sound ("Woof!") instead of the generic animal sound.

Why Inheritance Matters

- **Code Reusability:** You don't have to rewrite the same code for each class. Child classes automatically get the properties and methods of their parents.
- **Extensibility:** You can easily create new classes that build upon existing ones, adding specialized features or behaviors.
- **Organization:** Inheritance creates a clear hierarchy of classes, making your codebase more structured and easier to understand.

By mastering the concepts of `extends`, `super`, and method overriding, you can leverage the power of inheritance to create more organized, efficient, and flexible JavaScript code. Inheritance is a cornerstone of object-oriented programming and a powerful tool for modeling real-world relationships within your applications.

Code Examples of Inheritance in Action

Let's dive into practical examples that showcase the power of inheritance in JavaScript:

Example 1: Animals and Dogs

```
class Animal { // Parent Class
  constructor(name) {
    this.name = name;
  }

  speak() {
    console.log(this.name + " makes a sound.");
  }
}

class Dog extends Animal { // Child Class
  constructor(name, breed) {
    super(name);
    this.breed = breed;
  }

  speak() {
    console.log(this.name + " barks!"); // Overriding parent method
  }
}

const myDog = new Dog("Buddy", "Golden Retriever");
myDog.speak(); // Output: "Buddy barks!"
```

In this classic example, we have an `Animal` class with a generic `speak` method. The Dog class inherits from `Animal` using `extends`. Dog overrides the `speak` method to provide a specific behavior: barking. Notice how `super(name)` calls the parent constructor to ensure `name` is properly initialized.

Example 2: Vehicles and Cars

```
class Vehicle { // Parent Class
  constructor(brand, model) {
    this.brand = brand;
    this.model = model;
  }

  start() {
    console.log(`${this.brand} ${this.model} started!`);
  }
}

class Car extends Vehicle { // Child Class
  constructor(brand, model, year) {
    super(brand, model);
    this.year = year;
  }
```

```
  drive() {
    console.log(`Driving the ${this.year} ${this.brand} ${this.model}`);
  }
}

const myCar = new Car("Toyota", "Camry", 2023);
myCar.start(); // Output: "Toyota Camry started!" (inherited from Vehicle)
myCar.drive();  // Output: "Driving the 2023 Toyota Camry" (specific to Car)
```

The `Car` class inherits common properties (`brand`, `model`) and the `start` method from the `Vehicle` class. It adds its own `year` property and a `drive` method, demonstrating how child classes can extend functionality.

Example 3: Shapes and Rectangles

```
class Shape {
  constructor(color) {
    this.color = color;
  }

  describe() {
    console.log(`This is a ${this.color} shape.`);
  }
}

class Rectangle extends Shape {
  constructor(color, width, height) {
    super(color);
    this.width = width;
    this.height = height;
  }

  calculateArea() {
    return this.width * this.height;
  }
}

const myRectangle = new Rectangle("blue", 5, 10);
myRectangle.describe(); // Output: "This is a blue shape." (inherited)
console.log(myRectangle.calculateArea()); // Output: 50 (specific to
Rectangle)
```

Here, the `Rectangle` class inherits the `color` property and the `describe` method from `Shape`, showcasing how inheritance creates a hierarchy of related objects.

These examples demonstrate the essence of inheritance: the ability to create specialized classes that build upon existing ones, inheriting and extending properties and behaviors. This powerful feature promotes code reusability, modularity, and a logical structure for your JavaScript applications.

Polymorphism: Many Forms, One Interface

Polymorphism, a core principle of object-oriented programming (OOP), is the ability to treat objects of different classes interchangeably through a common interface. It's like a chameleon adapting to its environment, changing its appearance to fit in seamlessly. In JavaScript, this translates to objects having different internal structures but sharing the same external behavior.

The Power of Flexibility

Polymorphism empowers you to write code that is more generic and adaptable. Instead of writing separate functions for each specific type of object, you can create a single function that works with a variety of objects, as long as they share a common interface (a set of methods or properties with the same names).

Example: A Shape-Shifting Function

```
function printArea(shape) {
  console.log(`The area of this shape is: ${shape.calculateArea()}`);
}

const circle = new Circle(5);
const rectangle = new Rectangle(4, 6);

printArea(circle);     // Output: The area of this shape is: 78.53981633974483
printArea(rectangle); // Output: The area of this shape is: 24
```

In this example, the `printArea` function doesn't care if it receives a `Circle` or a `Rectangle`. As long as the object has a `calculateArea` method, the function can use it to get the area and print it. This demonstrates the power of polymorphism – you can write a single function that works with multiple object types, making your code more flexible and reusable.

Polymorphism and Inheritance

Polymorphism often goes hand in hand with inheritance. A child class can inherit a method from its parent class and provide its own unique implementation. This allows you to treat instances of the child class as if they were instances of the parent class, but with specialized behavior.

```
const animal = new Animal("Generic Animal");
const dog = new Dog("Buddy", "Golden Retriever");

animal.makeSound(); // Output: "Generic animal sound!"
dog.makeSound();    // Output: "Woof!"
```

Here, both `animal` and `dog` have a `makeSound` method, but they produce different results. This is polymorphism in action – the same method name, but different behavior depending on the object's type.

The Key to Generic Code

Polymorphism allows you to write more generic code by focusing on the common interface rather than the specific implementation. This makes your code more adaptable and easier to extend. For example, you could add a `Triangle` class with its own `calculateArea` method, and the `printArea` function would work seamlessly with it without any modifications.

By embracing polymorphism, you'll be able to write cleaner, more flexible, and more maintainable JavaScript code that can easily adapt to changing requirements and evolving object hierarchies.

Examples of Polymorphism in JavaScript

Let's dive into examples that showcase polymorphism in action within JavaScript, emphasizing how different classes can implement the same method with their own unique behavior:

Example 1: Shapes with `calculateArea()`

```
class Shape {
  constructor(name) {
    this.name = name;
  }

  calculateArea() {
    throw new Error("This method must be implemented by subclasses.");
  }
}

class Circle extends Shape {
  constructor(name, radius) {
    super(name);
    this.radius = radius;
  }

  calculateArea() {
    return Math.PI * this.radius ** 2;
  }
}

class Rectangle extends Shape {
  constructor(name, width, height) {
    super(name);
    this.width = width;
    this.height = height;
  }

  calculateArea() {
    return this.width * this.height;
  }
}

const circle = new Circle("Circle", 5);
const rectangle = new Rectangle("Rectangle", 4, 6);

console.log(circle.calculateArea());  // Output: 78.5398...
console.log(rectangle.calculateArea()); // Output: 24
```

In this example, the Shape class acts as the base class with a generic `calculateArea` method that throws an error if called directly. The `Circle` and `Rectangle` classes inherit from Shape and provide their own implementations of `calculateArea` to calculate the area specific to their shapes. This demonstrates polymorphism, as the same method name is used across different classes but behaves differently for each.

Example 2: Animals and their Sounds

```
class Animal {
  constructor(name) {
    this.name = name;
  }

  speak() {
```

```
    console.log("Generic animal sound!");
  }
}

class Dog extends Animal {
  speak() {
    console.log(this.name + " barks!");
  }
}

class Cat extends Animal {
  speak() {
    console.log(this.name + " meows!");
  }
}

const animals = [
  new Animal("Creature"),
  new Dog("Buddy"),
  new Cat("Whiskers")
];

animals.forEach(animal => animal.speak());
```

Here, `Dog` and `Cat` override the `speak` method inherited from `Animal`, providing their own unique sounds. The `forEach` loop demonstrates polymorphism by calling the same method (`speak`) on objects of different classes, resulting in different output for each animal.

Real-World Application: Rendering UI Elements

Imagine you are building a UI library with different types of elements like buttons, input fields, and checkboxes. Each element might have a `render` method that generates its HTML representation. Your framework could then have a generic `renderElement` function that takes any UI element object and simply calls its `render` method, regardless of the specific element type. This showcases polymorphism, as the same `render` method produces different HTML output depending on the specific element being rendered.

Chapter Summary

In this chapter, we explored how JavaScript embraces the principles of object-oriented programming (OOP) through its prototype-based inheritance model and the introduction of classes in ES6. We delved into the fundamental concepts of encapsulation, abstraction, inheritance, and polymorphism, demonstrating how they manifest in JavaScript.

We examined the structure of classes, including constructors, methods, class properties, and static methods, providing concrete examples of how to define and utilize them. We further explored inheritance, the ability to create new classes that inherit and extend functionality from existing classes, using the `extends` and `super` keywords and demonstrating how child classes can override inherited methods.

Finally, we illustrated the concept of polymorphism, highlighting its power in creating flexible and reusable code. We showcased examples where objects of different classes are treated interchangeably through a common interface, demonstrating how JavaScript enables you to write more generic functions that work with a variety of object types.

By mastering OOP principles and the features of classes in JavaScript, you have unlocked a powerful tool for building structured, maintainable, and extensible code. This knowledge will be invaluable as you tackle more complex projects and design scalable software solutions in JavaScript.

Section VI:
Putting it All Together

Real-World Applications: Case Studies and Project Ideas

Outline

- Applying JavaScript in Web Development
- Beyond the Browser: JavaScript's Expanding Reach
- Project Ideas: Putting Your Skills to the Test
- Chapter Summary

Applying JavaScript in Web Development

JavaScript has evolved into the powerhouse behind modern web experiences, breathing life into static HTML and CSS. Let's explore its diverse roles in shaping interactive and dynamic web applications:

1. Interactive UI Elements:

JavaScript injects interactivity into web pages, enabling elements that respond to user actions. This includes:

- **Drop-down Menus:** JavaScript shows and hides menus when users click or hover over a trigger element.
- **Image Sliders/Carousels:** JavaScript animates the transition between slides, handles user input for navigation, and manages timing.
- **Form Validation:** JavaScript checks user input for validity before submitting forms, ensuring data integrity and preventing errors.
- **Interactive Charts and Graphs:** JavaScript libraries like D3.js or Chart.js create visually appealing and dynamic charts that can update in real-time based on user input or changing data.

2. Dynamic Content Updates:

JavaScript's ability to fetch data asynchronously from servers (using technologies like AJAX or Fetch API) allows for dynamic content updates. This means you can update parts of a web page without reloading the entire page.

- **Loading More Content:** "Infinite scroll" websites use JavaScript to fetch and append new content as the user scrolls down.
- **Real-Time Updates:** Social media feeds, live chat applications, and stock tickers update dynamically using JavaScript to fetch new data periodically.
- **Personalized Content:** Websites can personalize content based on user preferences or behavior using JavaScript to fetch and display relevant information.

3. Single-Page Applications (SPAs):

SPAs are a modern architectural approach where the entire application is loaded once, and subsequent navigation and content updates happen within the same page. JavaScript handles all the routing, data fetching, and UI rendering, resulting in a smoother and faster user experience.

- **Examples:** Gmail, Google Maps, and many modern web applications are built as SPAs.

4. Front-End Frameworks: The Power Tools

JavaScript frameworks provide a structured way to build complex web applications. They offer pre-built components, tools, and patterns that streamline development and promote best practices.

- **React:** Developed by Facebook, known for its component-based architecture, virtual DOM, and declarative approach to UI updates.
- **Angular:** Developed by Google, a full-featured framework with powerful features like dependency injection, TypeScript integration, and a robust command-line interface (CLI).
- **Vue.js:** A progressive framework known for its flexibility, ease of learning, and gentle learning curve.

These frameworks leverage JavaScript's capabilities to create highly interactive, dynamic, and maintainable web applications.

By harnessing the power of JavaScript, you can transform static web pages into engaging and responsive experiences. Whether it's adding simple interactive elements, updating content dynamically, building full-fledged SPAs, or utilizing robust frameworks, JavaScript is the essential tool for creating the modern web.

Beyond the Browser: JavaScript's Expanding Reach

While JavaScript initially conquered the web browser, its versatility has led to a remarkable expansion into new territories, making it a true multi-platform language.

Server-Side Development (Node.js): JavaScript Takes the Backend

Node.js revolutionized the JavaScript landscape by bringing it to the server-side. At its core, Node.js is a runtime environment built on Chrome's V8 JavaScript engine. It empowers developers to create scalable network applications using JavaScript, the same language they use for front-end development.

Asynchronous Powerhouse

Node.js leverages JavaScript's asynchronous nature and event-driven model to handle concurrent requests efficiently. Instead of creating new threads for each request (as many server-side languages do), Node.js uses a single thread and an event loop to manage multiple requests simultaneously. This results in highly performant and scalable applications that can handle a large number of connections with minimal resource usage.

Versatility and Popularity

Node.js has become incredibly popular for building a wide range of server-side applications, including:

- **Web Servers and APIs:** Express.js, a popular Node.js framework, simplifies the creation of web servers and RESTful APIs.
- **Real-Time Applications:** Socket.IO, a library for real-time communication, allows you to build chat apps, collaborative tools, and other applications that require instant data exchange.
- **Microservices:** Node.js's lightweight nature and modularity make it ideal for building microservices, small, independent services that work together to form a larger application.

Mobile App Development (React Native): JavaScript Goes Mobile

React Native, built upon React, is a framework that allows developers to build native mobile apps for iOS and Android using JavaScript and a declarative UI paradigm.

The Bridge to Native

React Native doesn't produce web apps running in a WebView; instead, it translates your JavaScript code into native UI components. This means your app feels and performs like a native app, offering a smooth and responsive user experience.

Code Reusability

One of the most significant advantages of React Native is the ability to share a large portion of your codebase between iOS and Android platforms. This drastically reduces development time and effort, allowing you to build high-quality mobile apps more efficiently.

Growing Ecosystem

React Native boasts a thriving ecosystem of libraries and components, making it easier to build complex mobile apps with features like navigation, animations, and data persistence.

Desktop App Development (Electron): JavaScript on Your Desktop

Electron is a framework that enables you to build cross-platform desktop applications using the same technologies you use for the web: HTML, CSS, and JavaScript.

The Web Technologies Advantage

By leveraging web technologies, Electron allows you to create desktop applications that are visually appealing, highly customizable, and relatively easy to develop compared to traditional desktop development frameworks.

Popular Applications

Many popular applications are built with Electron, including Visual Studio Code, Slack, Discord, and Skype.

JavaScript's Ever-Expanding Reach

The journey of JavaScript from a browser scripting language to a versatile tool for server-side, mobile, and desktop development showcases its adaptability and the power of its underlying concepts. As JavaScript continues to evolve, we can expect even more exciting applications and possibilities in the years to come.

Project Ideas: Putting Your Skills to the Test

Ready to put your JavaScript skills to the test? Here are some exciting project ideas that will challenge you to apply the concepts you've learned throughout this book and unleash your creativity:

Web Development Projects

- **Interactive Quiz Game:**
  - Test your knowledge of scope, closures, and event handling by building a quiz game that dynamically loads questions, tracks the user's score, and provides feedback.
- **Weather App:**

    - Use `fetch` or `axios` to retrieve weather data from an API (e.g., OpenWeatherMap) and display it in a user-friendly format with icons, temperature, and forecasts.
- **To-Do List App:**
    - Build a classic to-do list application where users can add, edit, delete, and mark tasks as complete. Use local storage or a simple backend to persist the data.
- **Image Gallery:**
    - Create a visually appealing gallery that allows users to browse through images, view them in a lightbox, and add captions. Implement smooth navigation and transitions.
- **Interactive Map:**
    - Integrate a mapping library like Leaflet or Google Maps to create an interactive map with custom markers, overlays, and information windows. Allow users to search for locations and get directions.

Advanced Projects

- **Data Visualization:**
    - Fetch data from a CSV or JSON file and use charting libraries like D3.js or Chart.js to create informative and visually appealing visualizations, such as bar charts, line graphs, or scatter plots.
- **Chat Application:**
    - Build a real-time chat application using WebSockets or a similar technology. Implement features like user authentication, private messaging, and group chats.
- **Mini Game:**
    - Unleash your creativity and use JavaScript's canvas API to build a simple game like Snake, Pong, or Tetris. Explore game logic, animation, and user input handling.
- **Browser Extension:**
    - Extend the functionality of your favorite browser by creating a custom extension. Think of a task you want to automate or a feature you want to add, and bring it to life with JavaScript.

Your Own Unique Creations

Don't limit yourself to these suggestions! Think of problems you encounter in your daily life or tasks you want to automate. Use your imagination and newfound JavaScript skills to create your own unique applications.

Tips for Success

- **Start Small:** Begin with a simple project and gradually add complexity as you gain confidence.
- **Break Down the Problem:** Divide your project into smaller, manageable tasks.
- **Plan Your Structure:** Think about the overall architecture of your application and how the different components will interact.
- **Research Libraries and Tools:** Don't reinvent the wheel! Explore existing libraries and frameworks that can help you achieve your goals faster.
- **Test and Debug:** Thoroughly test your code and use debugging tools to identify and fix errors.
- **Seek Feedback:** Share your project with others and get feedback to improve your skills and your application.

Remember, the best way to learn is by doing. So, choose a project that excites you and start building! By applying the concepts and techniques covered in this book, you'll be amazed at what you can create with JavaScript.

Chapter Summary

In this chapter, we explored the vast landscape of real-world applications for JavaScript, both within and beyond the web browser. We saw how JavaScript empowers web developers to create interactive UI elements, dynamically update content, and build sophisticated single-page applications. We also ventured beyond the browser, discovering how JavaScript is used for server-side development with Node.js, mobile app development with React Native, and even desktop applications with Electron.

To solidify your learning, we provided a range of project ideas that challenge you to apply your JavaScript skills in practical ways. These projects cover various domains, from web development to data visualization, game development, and browser extensions. Remember, the possibilities are endless, and by experimenting with different projects, you'll continue to expand your knowledge and creativity as a JavaScript developer.

As you embark on your own JavaScript projects, keep in mind the concepts and techniques covered in this book. By mastering the quirks of JavaScript, understanding its object model, and applying functional programming principles, you'll be well-equipped to build robust, maintainable, and elegant applications that deliver exceptional user experiences.

Debugging and Troubleshooting: Tools and Strategies

Outline

The Art of Debugging

Debugging is a fundamental skill for any JavaScript developer. It's the process of systematically identifying and fixing errors in your code. Debugging isn't just about squashing bugs; it's about understanding how your code works, improving your problem-solving skills, and ultimately becoming a more proficient developer.

A Methodical Approach

Debugging is not a random guessing game. It's a methodical process that involves:

1. **Identifying the Problem:** What's the unexpected behavior or error message?
2. **Gathering Information:** What parts of your code are involved? What are the inputs and outputs?
3. **Formulating Hypotheses:** What might be causing the problem?
4. **Testing Hypotheses:** Experiment with changes to your code and observe the results.
5. **Iterating:** Repeat steps 3 and 4 until you've identified and fixed the issue.

Patience and Persistence

Debugging requires patience and a willingness to learn from your mistakes. Don't get discouraged by bugs; they're an inevitable part of the development process. Each bug you encounter is an opportunity to deepen your understanding of JavaScript and improve your coding skills.

General Debugging Tips

- **Reproduce the Problem:** Consistently reproducing the error is crucial. It helps you isolate the cause and test your fixes. If you can't reliably reproduce it, you'll have a hard time knowing if you've truly solved it.
- **Read Error Messages Carefully:** JavaScript error messages can be cryptic, but they often contain valuable information. Pay attention to the error type (e.g., `TypeError`, `ReferenceError`), the line number where it occurred, and any additional details provided.
- **The Scientific Method:** Apply the scientific method to debugging. Formulate a hypothesis about the cause of the bug, design an experiment (a code change) to test the hypothesis, and observe the results. If the problem persists, refine your hypothesis and try again.
- **Log and Trace:** Use `console.log()` statements or a debugger to track the flow of data through your code. This helps you pinpoint where values are incorrect or where the logic goes astray.
- **Isolate the Issue:** If you're dealing with a complex problem, try to break it down into smaller, more manageable parts. Focus on isolating the specific section of code that's causing the issue.

- **Don't Be Afraid to Ask for Help:** If you're stuck, don't hesitate to seek help from others. Ask a colleague, post on a forum like Stack Overflow, or search online for similar issues. Remember, even experienced developers get stuck sometimes!

By embracing a methodical approach, staying patient, and utilizing these debugging techniques, you can turn bugs into learning experiences and become a more proficient and confident JavaScript developer.

Essential Debugging Tools

Debugging is an art, and like any artist, you need the right tools to create a masterpiece. In the world of JavaScript, there's a rich set of tools to aid you in your bug-hunting endeavors. Let's explore some essentials that every JavaScript developer should have in their toolkit:

Browser Developer Tools: Your In-Browser Laboratory

Modern web browsers come equipped with powerful developer tools that offer a treasure trove of debugging features. Two of the most important tools for JavaScript debugging are:

- **The Console:** This is your command center for logging messages, inspecting variables, and evaluating JavaScript expressions in real-time. Use `console.log()` to print values to the console, `console.error()` for errors, and `console.warn()` for warnings.
- **The Debugger:** The debugger allows you to pause your code execution at specific points (breakpoints) and step through it line by line. You can inspect variables, watch their values change, and evaluate expressions to understand the flow of your code and pinpoint where errors occur.

Beyond the console and debugger, browser developer tools offer a wealth of other features:

- **Elements Panel:** Inspect and modify HTML elements and CSS styles directly in the browser.
- **Network Panel:** Analyze network requests and responses to track down issues with fetching data or communicating with APIs.
- **Performance Panel:** Identify performance bottlenecks in your JavaScript code and optimize loading times.

Code Editors with Debuggers: Your Coding Command Center

Modern code editors like Visual Studio Code, WebStorm, and Sublime Text offer integrated debugging features that make debugging a more streamlined experience. You can set breakpoints, step through code, inspect variables, and evaluate expressions all within the familiar environment of your editor.

These integrated debuggers often provide a more intuitive and user-friendly interface compared to browser developer tools, making them a popular choice for many developers.

Linters and Formatters: Automated Code Quality Assurance

Linters (like ESLint) and formatters (like Prettier) are automated tools that analyze your code and help you catch potential errors, enforce coding standards, and maintain consistent style.

- **Linters:** These tools scan your code for syntax errors, potential bugs (like unused variables), and deviations from best practices. They can be configured to enforce specific style guidelines and help you write cleaner and more reliable code.
- **Formatters:** Formatters automatically format your code to a consistent style, saving you time and ensuring readability.

By integrating linters and formatters into your development workflow, you can catch errors early, improve code quality, and reduce the amount of manual debugging required.

Online Debugging Tools: Quick and Convenient

Online debugging tools like JS Bin and CodePen are excellent for quickly testing and sharing code snippets. They provide a browser-based environment where you can write, run, and debug JavaScript code without the need for setting up a local development environment.

These tools are particularly useful for:

- **Collaboration:** Easily share your code with others for feedback or troubleshooting.
- **Prototyping:** Quickly test out ideas and experiment with new techniques.
- **Learning:** See how different code snippets behave in isolation.

By leveraging these essential debugging tools and incorporating them into your workflow, you'll be well-equipped to tackle even the most challenging JavaScript bugs and errors, ultimately leading to a smoother and more productive development experience.

Common JavaScript Errors and How to Fix Them

Common JavaScript Errors and How to Fix Them:

1. Syntax Errors

Syntax errors are the most basic and, thankfully, often the easiest type of error to catch in JavaScript. They occur when you violate the grammatical rules of the language. Think of them like typos or grammatical errors in a sentence.

Common Culprits:

- **Typos:** Incorrectly spelled keywords, variable names, or function names.
- **Missing or Mismatched Brackets, Braces, or Parentheses:** These can disrupt the structure of your code and confuse the JavaScript engine.
- **Missing Semicolons:** While JavaScript's automatic semicolon insertion (ASI) can sometimes help, it's best practice to include semicolons explicitly.
- **Incorrect Use of Quotes:** Using single quotes (') where you intended double quotes (") or vice versa.

Examples and Solutions

1. **Typo in Keyword:**

   ```
   functin myFunction() { // Typo in 'function'
     // ...
   }
   ```

   Solution: Carefully review the error message, which usually points to the line with the typo. In this case, correct "functin" to "function".

2. **Missing Curly Brace:**

   ```
   if (x > 5) {
     console.log("x is greater than 5");
   // Missing closing curly brace here
   ```

   Solution: The error message might indicate an "Unexpected end of input." Add the missing closing curly brace } to the end of the `if` block.

3. **Mismatched Parentheses:**

```
console.log("Hello" (world); // Mismatched parentheses: ( instead of )
```

Solution: Correct the mismatched parentheses to `console.log("Hello", world);`.

4. **Missing Semicolon:**

```
let x = 5
let y = 10

console.log(x + y); // Might work due to ASI, but best practice to add
semicolon
```

Solution: Add a semicolon after the declaration of y.

Tools to the Rescue

Modern code editors and linters like ESLint can often catch syntax errors before you even run your code. They provide real-time feedback, highlighting issues and suggesting fixes, making debugging a breeze.

Tips for Avoiding Syntax Errors

- **Proofread Your Code:** Carefully review your code for typos and missing punctuation.
- **Use a Linter:** Integrate a linter like ESLint into your development environment to automatically catch syntax errors.
- **Format Your Code:** Use a code formatter like Prettier to ensure consistent indentation and formatting, making errors easier to spot.
- **Test in Small Chunks:** Write and test your code in small increments, rather than trying to write a large block of code all at once.

By following these tips and utilizing the right tools, you can minimize syntax errors and ensure that your JavaScript code is well-formed and ready to execute.

2. Reference Errors

Reference errors occur when you try to use a variable or function that JavaScript can't find in the current scope or any of its parent scopes. It's like trying to enter a room that doesn't exist in your house of code.

Common Causes:

- **Undeclared Variables:** You're using a variable that hasn't been declared with `var`, `let`, or `const`.
- **Scope Issues:** The variable or function exists, but it's not accessible in the current scope due to being declared in a different scope.
- **Typos:** Misspelled variable or function names.

Examples and Solutions:

1. **Undeclared Variable:**

```
console.log(myVariable); // ReferenceError: myVariable is not defined
```

- **Solution:** Declare the variable before using it: `let myVariable = 10;`

2. **Scope Issue (Local Variable):**

```
function myFunction() {
  let secretMessage = "Hello from inside!";
}
```

```
console.log(secretMessage); // ReferenceError: secretMessage is not
defined
```

- **Solution:** You can't access `secretMessage` outside of `myFunction()`. Move the variable declaration outside the function to make it global, or return it from the function to use it elsewhere.

3. **Scope Issue (Block-Scoped Variable):**

```
if (true) {
  const blockVar = "I'm block-scoped!";
}
console.log(blockVar); // ReferenceError: blockVar is not defined
```

- **Solution:** Block-scoped variables (`let` and `const`) are not accessible outside their block. Move the declaration outside the block or restructure your code to access the variable within its scope.

4. **Typo:**

```
function sayHello(name) {
  console.log("Hello, " + nme + "!"); // Typo in 'name'
}
```

- **Solution:** Double-check variable and function names for typos. The error message usually indicates the misspelled identifier.

Best Practices to Avoid Reference Errors:

- **Declare Variables Before Use:** Always declare variables using `var`, `let`, or `const` before attempting to use them.
- **Check Scope:** Be mindful of where you declare your variables and functions. Make sure they are accessible in the scope where you're trying to use them.
- **Use a Linter:** Linters like ESLint can help catch undeclared variables and other scope-related issues before you run your code.
- **Use the Browser Console:** The browser console is a powerful tool for debugging. It often provides more detailed error messages and stack traces that can help you pinpoint the exact location of the reference error.

By understanding the causes of reference errors and following these best practices, you can significantly reduce the number of these errors in your JavaScript code. Remember, careful attention to detail and a structured debugging approach will help you quickly identify and fix any reference errors that do arise.

3. Type Errors

Type errors are a common stumbling block in JavaScript due to its dynamic typing system. They occur when you try to perform an operation on a value that is not of the expected data type. This could be trying to call a method on a number, accessing properties of `undefined`, or performing mathematical operations on strings.

Understanding Type Errors: Mismatched Expectations

In JavaScript, you might not explicitly declare a variable's type, but certain operations expect specific types. When these expectations aren't met, a type error is thrown.

Common Type Errors and Their Solutions

1. **Calling a Method on a Non-Function Object:**

```
const age = 30;
age.toUpperCase(); // TypeError: age.toUpperCase is not a function
```

- **Explanation:** The `toUpperCase()` method is designed for strings, not numbers.
- **Solution:** Convert the number to a string first: `age.toString().toUpperCase()`.

2. **Accessing Properties of `undefined` or `null`:**

```
let user; // undefined
console.log(user.name); // TypeError: Cannot read properties of undefined
(reading 'name')

let data = null;
console.log(data.length); // TypeError: Cannot read properties of null
(reading 'length')
```

- **Explanation:** `undefined` and `null` are not objects and don't have properties.
- **Solution:** Use conditional checks to ensure the variable is defined and not null before accessing its properties: `if (user) console.log(user.name);`.

3. **Mathematical Operations on Strings:**

```
const result = "5" + 2;
console.log(result); // Output: "52" (string concatenation)

const result2 = "hello" * 3;
console.log(result2); // Output: NaN (Not a Number)
```

- **Explanation:** The + operator is overloaded in JavaScript. It performs addition with numbers but concatenation with strings. Other arithmetic operators on strings usually result in NaN.
- **Solution:** Convert strings to numbers using `parseInt()` or `parseFloat()` before performing arithmetic operations, or use template literals for string interpolation.

Best Practices for Avoiding Type Errors:

- **Use `typeof` to Check Data Types:**

```
if (typeof myVariable === 'number') {
  // Perform operations specific to numbers
}
```

- **Validate Function Arguments:**

```
function greet(name) {
  if (typeof name !== 'string') {
    throw new TypeError('Name must be a string');
  }
  // ...
}
```

- **Use TypeScript:** Consider using TypeScript, a statically typed superset of JavaScript, to catch type errors during development.

By understanding the different types of errors and their solutions, you can confidently debug your JavaScript code. Remember, practice and the use of debugging tools will help you master the art of troubleshooting and ensure your code runs smoothly.

4. Range Errors

Range errors occur when you attempt to access an array element at an index that does not exist. In JavaScript, arrays are zero-indexed, meaning valid indices range from 0 to the array's length minus 1.

Understanding Range Errors: Out of Bounds Access

If you try to access an element at an index that is either negative or greater than or equal to the array's length, a RangeError is thrown, indicating that you are trying to access a value that is out of the allowed range.

Examples and Solutions:

1. **Negative Index:**

```
const numbers = [10, 20, 30];
console.log(numbers[-1]); // RangeError: Invalid array length
```

- **Explanation:** Arrays start at index 0, so negative indices are invalid.
- **Solution:** Ensure that your index is within the valid range (0 to 2 in this case).

2. **Index Exceeds Array Length:**

```
const fruits = ["apple", "banana", "orange"];
console.log(fruits[3]); // undefined (no error, but value is undefined)
```

- **Explanation:** The `fruits` array has a length of 3, so valid indices are 0, 1, and 2. Accessing `fruits[3]` does not throw an error but returns `undefined` because the element does not exist.
- **Solution:** Always check if the index is within the valid range before accessing an element.

```
if (index >= 0 && index < fruits.length) {
  console.log(fruits[index]);
} else {
  console.log("Invalid index");
}
```

Best Practices to Avoid Range Errors:

- **Check Array Length:** Before accessing an array element, always check if the index is within the valid range.
- **Use Array Methods:** Utilize array methods like `find`, `findIndex`, or `some` to safely search for elements or check for their existence before accessing them directly.
- **Handle Edge Cases:** Be mindful of situations where arrays might be empty or where indices are dynamically calculated. Add checks to prevent range errors in these cases.

By being vigilant about array indexing and implementing these best practices, you can effectively prevent range errors and ensure your JavaScript code runs smoothly. Remember, proper validation and careful attention to array boundaries will save you from unexpected errors and crashes.

5. **Logical Errors

Logical errors are the trickiest type of errors to catch because they don't cause your JavaScript code to crash. Instead, they silently produce incorrect or unexpected results due to flaws in your reasoning or algorithm. These errors can be particularly frustrating to debug, but with a systematic approach and the right tools, you can track them down and fix them.

Unmasking the Culprits:

- **Incorrect Calculations:** Mathematical errors, incorrect formulas, or miscalculations in your logic.
- **Flawed Comparisons:** Using the wrong comparison operator or incorrect conditions in your `if` statements or loops.
- **Incorrect Data Handling:** Misinterpreting or mishandling data from APIs, user input, or databases.

- **Algorithm Errors:** Implementing an algorithm incorrectly, leading to unexpected output or behavior.

Examples and Solutions:

1. **Incorrect Calculation:**

```
function calculateDiscount(price, discountPercentage) {
  const discountAmount = price * discountPercentage / 100;
  return price - discountAmount; // Should be price + discountAmount
}

const originalPrice = 100;
const discount = 10;
const finalPrice = calculateDiscount(originalPrice, discount);
console.log(finalPrice); // Output: 90 (incorrect)
```

- **Explanation:** The `calculateDiscount` function has a logical error in the calculation. It subtracts the discount amount instead of adding it.
- **Solution:** Correct the calculation to `return price + discountAmount;`

2. **Flawed Comparison:**

```
function checkAge(age) {
  if (age < 18) { // Should be age >= 18
    return "You are not eligible to vote.";
  } else {
    return "You are eligible to vote.";
  }
}
```

- **Explanation:** The `checkAge` function uses the wrong comparison operator, leading to incorrect eligibility results.
- **Solution:** Change the comparison to age >= 18 to check if the age is greater than or equal to 18.

3. **Incorrect Data Handling:**

```
const userData = { name: "Alice", age: "30" }; // Age is a string

if (userData.age > 18) {
  console.log("Adult");
} else {
  console.log("Minor");
} // Output: "Minor" (incorrect)
```

- **Explanation:** The age property is a string, and comparing a string with a number using > can lead to unexpected results due to type coercion.
- **Solution:** Convert the age to a number before the comparison:

```
if (parseInt(userData.age, 10) >= 18) {
  // ...
}
```

Best Practices for Avoiding Logical Errors:

- **Code Review:** Have someone else review your code for logic errors. A fresh perspective can often spot mistakes you might have missed.

- **Write Unit Tests:** Write tests to verify that your functions and algorithms produce the expected output for various input values.
- **Use a Debugger:** Step through your code using a debugger to track variable values and observe the flow of execution.
- **Modularize Your Code:** Break down your code into smaller, more manageable functions. This makes it easier to isolate and test individual pieces of logic.
- **Simplify Your Logic:** Complex logic is more prone to errors. Try to simplify your algorithms and conditional statements whenever possible.

Remember, logical errors are often the most challenging to find and fix. However, by employing a systematic approach, using the right tools, and adopting best practices, you can reduce the likelihood of these errors and build more reliable JavaScript applications.

Advanced Debugging Techniques

When faced with tricky bugs or performance issues that defy traditional debugging methods, it's time to level up your skills with advanced techniques. These techniques can help you pinpoint elusive errors and optimize your JavaScript code for better performance.

1. Remote Debugging: Bridging the Device Gap

Sometimes, you need to debug your JavaScript code as it runs in a different environment than your local development machine. This is where remote debugging comes in.

How It Works:

Remote debugging tools allow you to connect your development environment to a remote browser, device, or Node.js process. You can then use your familiar debugging tools (breakpoints, variable inspection, stepping through code) as if the code were running locally.

Tools and Tips:

- **Browser Developer Tools:** Most modern browsers offer remote debugging capabilities for mobile devices.
- **Remote Debugging Extensions:** Editors like VS Code and WebStorm provide extensions for remote debugging.
- **Node.js Debugging:** Node.js has built-in debugging capabilities using the `--inspect` flag. You can then connect a debugger client (like VS Code) to the running Node.js process.

2. Debugging Asynchronous Code: Taming the Timing Beast

Asynchronous code can be challenging to debug due to its non-linear nature. Here are some strategies:

- **`debugger` Statement:** Place `debugger` statements within your Promises, `async` functions, or callback functions to trigger a breakpoint when the debugger encounters them.
- **Browser Developer Tools Timeline:** The timeline view in browser developer tools can visualize the sequence of asynchronous events and help you pinpoint where things go wrong.
- **Promise Inspection:** Browser dev tools allow you to inspect the state (pending, fulfilled, rejected) and values of Promises.
- **Async Stack Traces:** Some browsers offer enhanced stack traces for asynchronous operations, showing the chain of function calls leading to the error.

3. Profiling: Finding Performance Bottlenecks

Profiling is the process of analyzing your code's performance to identify parts that are slowing it down. Profiling tools can help you pinpoint functions that take too long to execute, memory-hungry operations, or areas where the UI is being updated unnecessarily.

Tools and Tips:

- **Browser Performance Profiler:** The performance panel in browser dev tools provides profiling capabilities.
- **Node.js Profiling Tools:** Node.js has built-in profilers and also supports third-party tools.

4. Memory Leak Detection: Plugging the Leaks

Memory leaks occur when your JavaScript code holds on to objects in memory that are no longer needed. Over time, these leaks can accumulate and degrade your application's performance.

Tools and Tips:

- **Browser Memory Profiler:** The memory panel in browser dev tools can help you identify objects that are not being garbage collected.
- **Heap Snapshots:** Taking heap snapshots at different points in time allows you to compare object counts and detect leaks.
- **Memory Profiling Libraries:** Libraries like `memwatch-next` for Node.js can help you monitor memory usage and detect leaks.

Putting It All Together

Debugging is a multi-faceted skill that involves a combination of tools, techniques, and a systematic approach. By mastering advanced techniques like remote debugging, asynchronous code debugging, profiling, and memory leak detection, you'll be equipped to tackle even the most complex JavaScript challenges. Remember, effective debugging is not just about fixing bugs; it's about gaining a deeper understanding of your code and the runtime environment, ultimately leading to more robust and performant applications.

Chapter Summary

In this chapter, we delved into the art of debugging and troubleshooting JavaScript code, acknowledging that errors are an inevitable part of the development process. We emphasized the importance of a methodical approach, patience, and a willingness to learn from mistakes.

We explored essential tools like browser developer tools, code editors with integrated debuggers, linters, and online debugging platforms. These tools provide you with a powerful arsenal to identify and fix a wide range of issues.

We then examined common JavaScript errors, including syntax errors, reference errors, type errors, range errors, and logical errors. For each type of error, we provided clear explanations, code examples, and practical solutions to help you resolve them effectively.

Finally, we explored advanced debugging techniques, such as remote debugging for tackling issues on different devices or browsers, strategies for debugging asynchronous code, profiling for identifying performance bottlenecks, and memory leak detection to maintain your application's health.

By mastering these debugging tools and techniques, you can confidently troubleshoot even the most complex JavaScript errors, leading to cleaner, more reliable, and more performant code.

The Future of JavaScript: ESNext Features and Trends

Outline

- The Ever-Evolving JavaScript Landscape
- Notable ESNext Features
- Current Trends in the JavaScript Ecosystem
- Staying Ahead of the Curve
- Chapter Summary

The Ever-Evolving JavaScript Landscape

JavaScript, unlike some of its more static counterparts, is a living language that's continuously evolving. It's a testament to its adaptability and the passionate community of developers who constantly push its boundaries. At the heart of this evolution is the ECMAScript (ES) standard, a set of specifications maintained by the TC39 committee.

The ESNext Frontier

ESNext is the term used to refer to the upcoming JavaScript features that are not yet part of the official standard. These features are in various stages of development, ranging from early proposals to near-finalization. By keeping a pulse on ESNext, you gain a glimpse into the future of JavaScript and can start experimenting with cutting-edge features before they become widely adopted.

The Power of Staying Current

Why should you care about ESNext? Here are some compelling reasons:

- **Cleaner and More Expressive Code:**
    - ESNext features often introduce new syntax and capabilities that can streamline your code, making it more concise, readable, and expressive. For example, features like optional chaining and nullish coalescing operators eliminate the need for verbose null checks, enhancing code clarity.
- **Staying Ahead of the Curve:**
    - By adopting ESNext features, you position yourself at the forefront of JavaScript development. You'll be using the latest tools and techniques, demonstrating your commitment to modern best practices.
- **Future-Proofing Your Code:**
    - Browser vendors and JavaScript engines are constantly evolving. Staying current with ESNext helps ensure your code remains compatible with future updates. You won't be caught off guard when new features become standard and older ones are deprecated.

A Glimpse into the Future

Some of the most exciting ESNext features include:

- **Record and Tuple:** These provide immutable data structures for better data integrity and easier reasoning about state.
- **Pattern Matching:** This feature simplifies complex conditional logic, making your code more concise and easier to follow.

- **Pipeline Operator:** This operator enhances code readability by allowing you to chain operations in a more natural way.
- **Temporal API:** This provides a modern and comprehensive way to work with dates and times in JavaScript.
- **Decorators:** These enable you to add metadata and modify the behavior of classes, methods, and properties.

By staying informed about ESNext and experimenting with these new features, you'll be well-prepared to leverage the full power of JavaScript as it continues to evolve.

Notable ESNext Features

The JavaScript landscape is constantly evolving, with new features and proposals on the horizon. These ESNext additions promise to enhance the language's expressiveness, safety, and overall developer experience. Let's explore some of the most noteworthy ESNext features:

1. Pattern Matching: Concise and Expressive Logic

Pattern matching is a powerful construct that simplifies complex conditional logic by allowing you to match values against patterns and extract relevant parts.

```
// Before pattern matching
function httpResponse(status) {
  if (status === 200) {
    return "OK";
  } else if (status === 404) {
    return "Not Found";
  } else {
    return "Unknown Status";
  }
}

// With pattern matching
function httpResponse(status) {
  return match(status) {
    case 200 => "OK";
    case 404 => "Not Found";
    _ => "Unknown Status"; // _ is the wildcard pattern
  }
}
```

Pattern matching makes your code more concise and readable, especially when dealing with multiple possible cases.

2. Records and Tuples: Immutable Data Structures

- **Records:** Immutable objects with a fixed set of keys. This guarantees that the object's structure cannot be changed after creation, improving predictability and safety.

  ```
  const point = #{ x: 3, y: 5 }; // # denotes a record
  // point.x = 10; // Error: Records are immutable
  ```

- **Tuples:** Immutable ordered lists of values. They are useful for representing fixed-size collections of data where the order matters.

  ```
  const person = #["Alice", 30, "Engineer"]; // # denotes a tuple
  ```

```
// person[1] = 35; // Error: Tuples are immutable
```

Records and tuples bring immutability to JavaScript, making your code easier to reason about and reducing the risk of bugs due to unintended data modification.

3. Temporal API: Dates and Times Done Right

The Temporal API is a new, modern way to work with dates and times in JavaScript. It provides a comprehensive set of classes and methods for handling time zones, calendars, durations, and more.

```
const now = Temporal.Now.instant();
const later = now.add({ hours: 3 });
console.log(later.toString());
```

The Temporal API addresses many of the pain points and inconsistencies of the older `Date` object, making date and time manipulation more reliable and intuitive.

4. Pipeline Operator: Streamlined Chaining

The pipeline operator (|>) allows you to chain operations together in a more readable and natural flow.

```
const result = value
  |> double
  |> increment
  |> square;
```

This is equivalent to `square(increment(double(value)))`, but it's much easier to read from left to right. (Note that browser support for the pipeline operator is still experimental.)

5. Decorators: Enhancing Classes and Functions

Decorators are a proposed feature that allows you to add metadata to classes, methods, and properties. They can be used for various purposes, such as:

- Logging: Automatically log function calls.
- Validation: Validate input data for a class or method.
- Caching: Cache results of expensive function calls.

```
@log // Decorator for logging function calls
function myFunction(arg) {
  // ...
}
```

Decorators can enhance the functionality of your code in a clean and declarative way.

By staying informed about these ESNext features and exploring their capabilities, you can leverage the latest advancements in JavaScript to write more efficient, expressive, and robust code. Remember, the JavaScript language is always evolving, and embracing new features can help you stay ahead of the curve and build cutting-edge applications.

Current Trends in the JavaScript Ecosystem

The JavaScript ecosystem is a dynamic and ever-changing landscape. New tools, libraries, and frameworks emerge regularly, while existing ones evolve to meet the demands of modern web development. Let's explore some of the major trends shaping the JavaScript ecosystem in 2024 and beyond.

TypeScript's Rise: The Static Typing Revolution

TypeScript, a statically typed superset of JavaScript developed by Microsoft, has experienced a meteoric rise in popularity in recent years. By adding static types to JavaScript, TypeScript provides a number of benefits, especially for large-scale projects:

- **Improved Code Quality:** Static types help catch errors during development, reducing bugs and improving code reliability.
- **Enhanced Tooling:** TypeScript offers excellent tooling support, including code completion, type checking, and refactoring tools, making development more efficient.
- **Better Collaboration:** Static types make it easier for teams to work together on large codebases, as they provide a clear contract for function inputs and outputs.

While TypeScript might not be suitable for all projects, it's increasingly becoming the go-to choice for enterprise-level applications and projects that require a high degree of predictability and maintainability.

Functional Programming Influence: The Rise of Pure Functions and Immutability

Functional programming (FP) continues to exert a significant influence on the JavaScript ecosystem. Libraries like Ramda and Lodash provide a rich set of tools for functional programming in JavaScript, and developers are increasingly embracing concepts like pure functions, immutability, and function composition.

This trend is driven by the desire for cleaner, more predictable, and easier-to-reason-about code. By avoiding side effects and relying on immutable data, functional programming can lead to more reliable and testable applications.

WebAssembly (WASM): The Performance Powerhouse

WebAssembly (WASM) is a binary instruction format that can be executed in web browsers alongside JavaScript. It's designed to be fast, efficient, and portable, allowing you to run computationally intensive tasks like gaming, 3D graphics, and scientific simulations at near-native speed within the browser.

While WASM is still in its early stages, it has the potential to revolutionize web development by enabling high-performance applications that were previously not feasible. As WASM adoption grows, we can expect to see more and more web apps pushing the boundaries of what's possible in the browser.

Serverless Architecture: The Cloud-Native Way

Serverless architecture is a cloud computing model where developers can deploy code as functions that are executed in response to events (like HTTP requests or database changes). This eliminates the need to manage servers directly, allowing you to focus on writing your application logic.

JavaScript, with its event-driven nature and asynchronous capabilities, is a perfect fit for serverless architectures. Platforms like AWS Lambda, Google Cloud Functions, and Azure Functions offer seamless integration with JavaScript, making it easy to deploy and scale your applications.

JAMstack (JavaScript, APIs, Markup): The Modern Web Architecture

JAMstack is a modern web architecture that emphasizes pre-rendering and decoupling. Instead of generating pages dynamically on the server, JAMstack sites are pre-rendered into static HTML files, which can be served from a CDN (Content Delivery Network). Dynamic functionality is then added using JavaScript and APIs.

This approach offers numerous benefits:

- **Performance:** Static files are served quickly from a CDN, resulting in faster page load times.

- **Security:** Static files are less vulnerable to attacks than dynamic server-rendered pages.
- **Scalability:** CDNs can easily handle high traffic loads.
- **Developer Experience:** JAMstack sites are often easier to develop and deploy than traditional server-rendered applications.

By staying informed about these current trends and embracing the technologies that resonate with you, you can leverage the ever-evolving JavaScript ecosystem to build cutting-edge web applications that are performant, scalable, and secure. The future of JavaScript is bright, and by staying ahead of the curve, you can unlock new possibilities for your projects and your career.

Staying Ahead of the Curve

The JavaScript world is constantly evolving, with new features and tools emerging regularly. To stay ahead of the curve and leverage the latest advancements, you need to adopt a mindset of continuous learning and experimentation. Here's your roadmap to staying current:

Following TC39 Proposals: The Path to Standardization

TC39 is the committee responsible for evolving the ECMAScript (ES) standard, which defines the JavaScript language. They maintain a public repository of proposals for new features, each with a defined stage of maturity:

- **Stage 0: Strawperson:** An initial idea or suggestion.
- **Stage 1: Proposal:** A formal proposal with a champion (someone who is responsible for driving the proposal forward).
- **Stage 2: Draft:** A detailed specification for the feature.
- **Stage 3: Candidate:** The feature is nearly complete and ready for implementation in browsers and engines.
- **Stage 4: Finished:** The feature is included in the official ECMAScript standard.

By following the TC39 proposals, you can get an early look at upcoming features and understand the rationale behind their design. You can find the proposals on the official TC39 GitHub repository: https://github.com/tc39/proposals

Reading Blogs and Articles: Staying Informed

The JavaScript community is incredibly active, with countless blogs, articles, and newsletters dedicated to sharing the latest news, insights, and best practices. Here are a few reputable sources to follow:

- **JavaScript Weekly:** A weekly newsletter that curates the best JavaScript articles and news.
- **Smashing Magazine (JavaScript Section):** In-depth articles on various JavaScript topics, including ESNext features.
- **2ality Blog:** Dr. Axel Rauschmayer's blog, known for its deep dives into JavaScript internals and language features.
- **Official Blogs of Framework Authors:** Follow the blogs of your favorite framework creators (e.g., React, Vue.js, Angular) to stay up-to-date on their latest developments.

Experimenting with ESNext Features: Learn by Doing

The best way to understand new features is to use them! Don't be afraid to experiment with ESNext features in your projects, even if they aren't fully supported in all browsers yet. Tools like Babel allow you to transpile your code, converting it into a format that older browsers can understand.

By setting up a development environment that supports ESNext, you can get hands-on experience with new features and incorporate them into your workflow as soon as they become available. This proactive approach will keep your skills sharp and your code modern.

The Importance of Continuous Learning

The JavaScript ecosystem is constantly evolving, and the only way to stay ahead is to keep learning and experimenting. By following TC39 proposals, reading relevant blogs and articles, and actively trying out new features, you'll be well-equipped to build cutting-edge web applications and stay at the forefront of the JavaScript community.

Remember, the future of JavaScript is bright, and by embracing a mindset of continuous learning, you can unlock its full potential and build the next generation of web experiences.

Chapter Summary

In this chapter, we explored the ever-evolving landscape of JavaScript, emphasizing the importance of staying ahead of the curve. We learned about ESNext, the term for upcoming JavaScript features that are not yet part of the official standard. We discussed how keeping up with these features can lead to cleaner, more expressive code, ensure future compatibility, and position you at the forefront of web development.

We highlighted some notable ESNext features, including pattern matching, records and tuples, the Temporal API, the pipeline operator, and decorators. We discussed how each of these features can improve your code in different ways, from simplifying conditional logic to providing better tools for working with dates and times.

We also delved into current trends in the JavaScript ecosystem, such as the rise of TypeScript, the growing influence of functional programming, the potential of WebAssembly, and the shift towards serverless architecture and JAMstack. These trends are shaping the way we build web applications, and understanding them is crucial for staying relevant as a JavaScript developer.

Finally, we offered tips and resources for staying informed about the latest JavaScript features and trends. By following TC39 proposals, reading relevant blogs and articles, and experimenting with ESNext features, you can ensure that your skills remain sharp and your code up-to-date. Remember, the JavaScript landscape is constantly changing, and embracing a mindset of continuous learning and experimentation is key to mastering this versatile language.

Appendices

Appendix A1: JavaScript Resources: Books, Websites, and Communities

This appendix is your treasure trove for further exploration into the vast and dynamic world of JavaScript. Whether you're seeking deeper knowledge, practical examples, or community support, these resources will guide you on your journey to JavaScript mastery.

Books

- **"You Don't Know JS" series by Kyle Simpson:** This in-depth series dives into the core mechanisms of JavaScript, including scope, closures, `this`, types, and more. It's a must-read for anyone who wants to truly understand the language.
- **"Eloquent JavaScript" by Marijn Haverbeke:** This comprehensive book covers both the fundamentals and advanced concepts of JavaScript, with a focus on practical examples and exercises.
- **"JavaScript: The Good Parts" by Douglas Crockford:** A classic that focuses on the best practices and patterns in JavaScript, helping you write cleaner and more maintainable code.
- **"Secrets of the JavaScript Ninja" by John Resig, Bear Bibeault, and Josip Maras:** This book dives into advanced techniques, including cross-browser strategies, DOM scripting, and event handling.
- **"Effective JavaScript" by David Herman:** Packed with practical tips and insights for writing efficient and idiomatic JavaScript code.

Websites

- **MDN Web Docs (Mozilla Developer Network):** The definitive resource for web technologies, including comprehensive documentation on JavaScript, its APIs, and best practices.
- **JavaScript.info:** A beginner-friendly website with interactive tutorials and examples that cover JavaScript from scratch.
- **FreeCodeCamp:** A free online learning platform that offers a comprehensive JavaScript curriculum with hands-on projects.
- **Hackr.io (JavaScript Section):** A curated list of the best JavaScript tutorials, courses, and resources from around the web.
- **JavaScript Playground:** A website that allows you to experiment with JavaScript code directly in your browser.

Communities

- **Stack Overflow:** The go-to Q&A platform for developers. Ask questions, find solutions to common problems, and learn from others' experiences.
- **Reddit (r/javascript):** A subreddit dedicated to JavaScript news, discussions, and questions.
- **DEV Community (JavaScript Tag):** A platform where developers share articles, tutorials, and experiences related to JavaScript.
- **JavaScript Meetups and Conferences:** Attend local or online meetups and conferences to connect with fellow JavaScript enthusiasts, learn from experts, and stay up-to-date on the latest trends.

Additional Tips

- **Explore Libraries and Frameworks:** Dive into popular libraries like React, Angular, or Vue.js, and explore their documentation and examples.
- **Read Source Code:** Reading the source code of well-written JavaScript projects can be a valuable learning experience.
- **Contribute to Open Source:** Contribute to open-source JavaScript projects to gain experience and learn from other developers.
- **Practice, Practice, Practice:** The more you code, the better you'll become at JavaScript. Build projects, experiment with new features, and challenge yourself to solve problems.

Remember, learning is a continuous journey. By exploring these resources and engaging with the vibrant JavaScript community, you'll continue to grow as a developer and unlock the full potential of this powerful and versatile language.

Appendix A2: JavaScript Best Practices

In this appendix, we'll distill the wisdom accumulated by the JavaScript community into a set of best practices. These guidelines will help you write cleaner, more maintainable, and more efficient code that avoids common pitfalls and leverages the language's strengths.

Code Style and Formatting

- **Use Consistent Indentation:** Choose either spaces or tabs (but not both) and stick to a consistent indentation style throughout your codebase. This makes code easier to read and understand.
- **CamelCase for Variables and Functions:** Use camelCase for variable and function names (e.g., `firstName`, `calculateTotal`). This improves readability and follows common JavaScript conventions.
- **PascalCase for Classes:** Use PascalCase for class names (e.g., `MyClass`, `ShoppingCart`).
- **Meaningful Names:** Choose descriptive names for variables, functions, and classes that reflect their purpose. Avoid single-letter variables or cryptic abbreviations.
- **Comments:** Write clear and concise comments to explain the purpose and functionality of your code. Use JSDoc-style comments for documenting functions, classes, and modules.
- **Code Formatting Tools:** Utilize tools like Prettier to automatically format your code to a consistent style, saving you time and effort.

Language Features and Usage

- **Use `const` for Constants:** Declare variables that should not be reassigned with `const`. This helps prevent accidental changes to values.
- **Prefer `let` over `var`:** Use `let` for variables with block scope, as it avoids the potential issues associated with `var`'s function scope and hoisting.
- **Avoid Global Variables:** Minimize the use of global variables to prevent namespace pollution and unintended side effects. Instead, use modules or other encapsulation techniques to manage data.
- **Use Strict Equality (=== and !==):** Prefer strict equality operators to avoid unexpected type coercion in comparisons.
- **Arrow Functions:** Use arrow functions for cleaner syntax and lexical scoping of `this`.
- **Template Literals:** Leverage template literals for creating cleaner and more readable strings with embedded expressions.
- **Destructuring:** Use destructuring to extract values from arrays and objects in a concise way.
- **Spread and Rest Operators:** Utilize the spread (`...`) and rest (`...`) operators for array and object manipulation.
- **Modules (ES Modules):** Organize your code into modules for better maintainability and reusability.

Performance and Optimization

- **Minimize DOM Manipulation:** Direct DOM manipulation can be expensive. Use techniques like virtual DOM diffing to optimize updates.
- **Avoid Global Lookups:** Cache references to frequently accessed global variables or functions.
- **Use Efficient Data Structures:** Choose the right data structures (e.g., arrays, objects, maps, sets) for your specific use cases.
- **Lazy Loading:** Load resources like images or scripts only when they are needed to improve initial page load time.
- **Debouncing and Throttling:** Limit the rate at which functions are called in response to events like scrolling or resizing to avoid performance issues.

Error Handling and Testing

- **Use `try...catch` Blocks:** Handle potential errors gracefully using `try...catch` blocks.
- **Throw Custom Errors:** Create custom error classes for specific error scenarios in your application.
- **Write Unit Tests:** Write unit tests to verify the correctness of your code and catch regressions early in the development process.
- **Use a Testing Framework:** Use a testing framework like Jest or Mocha to automate your tests and make them easier to run and maintain.

Security

- **Sanitize User Input:** Always sanitize user input to prevent cross-site scripting (XSS) attacks and other vulnerabilities.
- **Validate Data:** Validate data from external sources to ensure it meets your expectations and is safe to use.
- **Use HTTPS:** Secure your website with HTTPS to protect user data and prevent tampering.

By adhering to these best practices, you'll be well on your way to writing high-quality, maintainable, and secure JavaScript code that adheres to industry standards and best practices.

Appendix A3: ES6+ Cheat Sheet: A Quick Reference for Modern Syntax

This cheat sheet is your quick reference guide to the most useful features introduced in ECMAScript 2015 (ES6) and later versions. It's designed to be a handy reference when you need a quick reminder of the syntax or a concise overview of how a particular feature works.

Variables

- `let` and `const`: Declare block-scoped variables (replace `var`). `const` declares constants.

```
let x = 5;  // Can be reassigned
const PI = 3.14159; // Cannot be reassigned
```

Arrow Functions

- Concise syntax for functions:

```
const add = (x, y) => x + y;
const square = x => x * x;
```

- Lexical `this` binding: Arrow functions automatically bind `this` to the surrounding context.

Destructuring

- Extract values from arrays or objects:

```
const [first, second] = [1, 2, 3];
const { name, age } = { name: "Alice", age: 30 };
```

Spread and Rest Syntax

- Spread (`...`): Expand arrays or objects into individual elements or properties.
- Rest (`...`): Collect multiple arguments into an array.

```
const numbers = [1, 2, 3];
const newNumbers = [...numbers, 4, 5]; // [1, 2, 3, 4, 5]

function myFunction(first, ...rest) {
  console.log(first); // First argument
  console.log(rest);   // Array of remaining arguments
}
```

Classes

- Define blueprints for creating objects:

```
class Person {
  constructor(name, age) {
    this.name = name;
    this.age = age;
```

```
  }

  greet() {
    console.log(`Hello, my name is ${this.name}.`);
  }
}
```

- `extends` for inheritance:

```
class Student extends Person {
  // ...
}
```

Modules (ES Modules)

- Export and import modules:

```
// math.js
export function add(x, y) {
  return x + y;
}

// main.js
import { add } from './math.js';
```

Template Literals

- Create strings with embedded expressions and multi-line support:

```
const name = "Bob";
const greeting = `Hello, ${name}!
Welcome to our website.`;
```

Promises and Async/Await

- Handle asynchronous operations:

```
async function fetchData() {
  try {
    const response = await fetch('https://api.example.com/data');
    const data = await response.json();
    console.log(data);
  } catch (error) {
    console.error("Error:", error);
  }
}
```

Default Parameters

- Provide default values for function parameters:

```
function greet(name = "World") {
  console.log(`Hello, ${name}!`);
}
```

Other ES6+ Features

- **Enhanced Object Literals:** Computed property names, shorthand method syntax.
- **Generators:** Functions that can be paused and resumed, useful for iterators and asynchronous code.
- **Maps and Sets:** New data structures for storing unique values and key-value pairs.
- **Symbols:** Unique and immutable identifiers.
- **Proxies:** Objects that can intercept and customize operations on other objects.

This cheat sheet is just a starting point. Many more features and refinements have been added to JavaScript since ES6. Always refer to the official ECMAScript documentation and other reliable resources for comprehensive information on specific features and their usage.

Conclusion

Congratulations! You've journeyed through the intricacies of JavaScript, exploring its quirks, mastering its building blocks, and delving into advanced concepts like closures, prototypes, asynchronous programming, and functional programming. You've even dipped your toes into the world of framework construction, learning the core principles and tools for creating your own JavaScript tools.

Embracing the Quirks

By now, you should have a deeper appreciation for JavaScript's unique features and behaviors. What might have seemed like quirks or inconsistencies at first are now tools you can wield to write more elegant, efficient, and expressive code. You understand how scope governs variable visibility, how closures capture state, and how prototypes enable inheritance. You've learned to tame the `this` keyword, harness the power of asynchronous programming, and appreciate the benefits of a functional programming mindset.

From Foundations to Mastery

This book has laid a solid foundation for your continued exploration of JavaScript. You now have the knowledge and confidence to tackle more advanced topics, delve into specialized libraries and frameworks, and even build your own JavaScript tools.

The Journey Never Ends

Remember, the world of JavaScript is constantly evolving. New features, libraries, and best practices emerge regularly. The key to continued success is to embrace a lifelong learning mindset. Stay curious, explore new resources, and experiment with different approaches.

Join the Community

The JavaScript community is vast and vibrant. Connect with other developers through online forums, meetups, and conferences. Share your knowledge, learn from others, and collaborate on exciting projects. The JavaScript ecosystem is a collaborative one, and by being an active participant, you'll accelerate your growth and contribute to the language's continued evolution.

Go Forth and Build

Armed with the knowledge and skills you've gained from this book, you are now ready to embark on your own JavaScript adventures. Build amazing applications, create innovative solutions, and contribute to the ever-growing world of JavaScript. The possibilities are limitless, and your journey has just begun.

---

www.ingramcontent.com/pod-product-compliance
Lightning Source LLC
Chambersburg PA
CBHW082107220526
45472CB00009B/2077

* 9 7 9 8 3 2 8 1 5 7 8 9 6 *